Praise for
The Warrior's Book of Virtues

"…a great reflection of wisdom through the eyes of self-less servants."

—Alejandro Villanueva,
Offensive Tackle for Pittsburgh Steelers,
U.S. Army Ranger and West Point alumnus

"You'll not find more qualified people to give advice on how to lead a life that matters."

—Dr. David Macpherson,
Professor of Medicine and Chief Medical Officer,
VISN4, Veterans Health Administration

"…provides the tools to build resilience and the faith in our own perspectives that can help to guide us along the way."

—Christine Moghadam,
CEO and Founder of Corc Yoga

"…exceptional fortitude, objectivity and personal insight."

—John Watters, DO,
Staff Physician, VA Pittsburgh

"These guys know what it takes to be a warrior, both on the battlefields of war and the battlefields of daily life."

—Jared Verrillo, serial entrepreneur

"…a must-read."

—Adam Greenberg,
motivational speaker

"Stick to the plan without compromise."

—Jeffrey Rodriguez, USMC

"Explore why virtue is vital by reading this book."

—Kate Deeks,
writing coach and founder of OMNES

THE
WARRIOR'S
BOOK OF
VIRTUES

THE
WARRIOR'S
BOOK OF
VIRTUES

A Field Manual for
Living Your Best Life

NICK BENAS, MATT BLOOM
and BUZZ BRYAN

Foreword by Ben Biddick
Preface by Stewart Smith, USN (SEAL)

THE WARRIOR'S BOOK OF VIRTUES

Text copyright © 2019 Nick Benas,
Matt Bloom and Buzz Bryan

Library of Congress Cataloging-in-Publication
Data is available upon request.
ISBN: 978-1-57826-807-8

COVER AND INTERIOR DESIGN BY CAROLYN KASPER

Printed in the United States
10 9 8 7 6 5 4 3 2 1

Dedication

To the memory of my late grandfather, James "Pap" Martin, USAF Retired. Your service to our country and family is the example I try to live by each day.

—Bloom

To my wife Chrissie and our three sons, Sean, Christian and Zach, for their unconditional support, love, and for believing in me. I have to also thank all who served in front of us, those who served with me, and those who have come after and are forward now. I am in awe of your selfless service to our nation.

—Buzz

To my family.

—Benas

…And, with gratitude, for Carol Welte Richmond, for her tireless help with in-depth interviews and her assistance with the writing process.

Contents

Authors' Note

"A spirit of comradeship and brotherhood in arms came into being in the training camps and on the battlefields. This spirit is too fine a thing to be allowed to die. It must be fostered and kept alive and made the moving force in all Marine Corps Organizations."
—MAJOR GENERAL A. LEJEUNE

A WARRIOR IS NOT defined by gender, culture, skin color, age, intellect, socio-economic status, generation, or political affiliation. A warrior is defined by the things they do, and their lifelong commitment to improvement. Becoming a warrior means embarking on an ever-evolving journey towards a destination of elite mental status—reaching a place where we can truly be our best selves.

We're all bombarded daily with chores, responsibilities, the demands of others, the demands we put on ourselves... a cacophony of inner and outer voices, each one striving to be heard. And oftentimes, the directives given by these voices are ones of service: simple, mundane and frequently boring tasks.

Service to yourself or a loved one, before you leave for work or school: *make your bed, brush your teeth, take a shower, use deodorant, eat breakfast, get dressed, feed the kids, pay the bills*...the list endless. Typically, when these tasks present themselves, we're tempted to respond with, *"Why?"* or, *"What's the point? Who cares?"*

There *are* valid answers to these questions—answers that offer a reason for and validity to making your bed, even when no one's looking. Our goal with this book is to help everyone see the long-term benefits of the daily rinse-and-repeat. To recognize these actions not as tests of our patience, but as signifiers of our diligence. In doing so, we hope to lead you along a path to success of your own choosing.

Our responsibility as warriors is to do battle, to make better decisions when called upon, and to cultivate just and virtuous lives. This is not always easy; for this reason, warriors are expected to adapt to less-than-desirable circumstances and overcome any obstacles standing in their way.

To those men and women who served in and out of the theatre of war, and to those who continue to serve, we thank you. Further, we understand how humble you are about your service, and that being referred to as a "warrior" might carry a deeper and even unsettling meaning. We recognize that for us to make close relatives of war and civilian life in our offering here can be just as jarring. Please know that we can relate: when someone refers to us as "soldiers," it makes our skin crawl. The titles "Marine" and "Sailor" exist at a fundamental level of our DNA, and for us to personally unpack why the label "soldier" bothers us could take a lifetime. The society we live in doesn't make things any easier: we've become collectively hypersensitive, as ordinary, mundane conversations among friends and family have to be interrupted and refereed when participants or even just observers get "triggered." People are afraid to share their honest thoughts and feelings because they're afraid of being "politically incorrect" or "touching on a sensitivity." The result is emotional and mental paralysis on a cultural level, as we suppress our thoughts in speech because we struggle mightily to listen and understand each other.

Our real hope is that the concepts woven into the pages of this book, upheld through centuries of humanity and borne out in the lives of countless incredible people, will serve as a source of inspiration and motivation. By sharing of our life experiences thus far, the successes and gains alongside the failures and losses, we hope to give you the confidence to eliminate unnecessary distractions and roadblocks so you can do what you need to do to create a virtue-driven life of freedom and happiness for yourself and a lasting legacy filled with pleasant memories for you and your loved ones.

With that said: a "warrior" is simply a catch-all term for an individual who specializes in the art of fighting and combat. And if you've picked up this book—if you're reading these words—you *are* a warrior. If you decide to embark on this journey with us, we ask you to embrace the bad and keep fighting the good fight, to eventually succeed at understanding and implementing the four cardinal virtues of temperance, prudence, fortitude and justice into your everyday life. Remember: warriors lead with virtue. We are on your side, and at your side; this is a path we all walk together.

The three of us bonded in the military while working together half a world away, in what now seems like a lifetime ago. It is a true example of mutual admiration, loyalty and respect that our friendship and consistent support for each other continues. We trust each other implicitly. We still hold each other accountable during the tough times. We don't share embellished glory stories in this book to impress or boast; nor do we make any claims of magnificent feats of heroism in these pages. We were just doing our jobs. We take our jobs very seriously, but all the same we try not to take life too seriously. We look forward to sharing with you glimpses of our authentic vulnerability, our personal fears, foibles and the forces at play that have held us back and propelled us forward. These experiences, without question, are what have made us the men we are today.

Foreword
by Ben Biddick

"Still I hope I shall always possess firmness and virtue enough to maintain (what I consider the most enviable of all titles) the character of an honest man."
  —GEORGE WASHINGTON

I WILL ALWAYS REMEMBER speaking with a United States Army soldier who worked in a Combat Support Hospital in Afghanistan during the Global War on Terror. He described his experiences caring for those who sustained tremendous injuries during combat operations and how the treatment of these people affected him as a caregiver.

He was particularly impacted by the unique experience of treating and stabilizing United States Marines. Upon receiving medical treatment, Marines would consistently vanish from the hospital before being discharged to return to their units, who were serving in the same combat that had resulted in their injury. It didn't matter what the Army medical officers ordered them to do; it didn't matter to these Marines if they were threatened with potentially being reported as AWOL, if there was a risk for infection, if they only had a partial or filthy uniform left, or if their gear was damaged and still covered with battlefield blood and sand. Their cohesion was so powerful that nothing stopped them from getting back to their units and accomplishing their mission.

Because of this conversation, I felt no surprise when I spoke with Nick Benas, Matt Bloom, and Richard "Buzz" Bryan about their book *The Warrior's Book of Virtues.* Nick and Matt were United States Marine Corps veterans who served in and around Ramadi, Fallujah, and Al Qaim in Iraq during the Global War on Terror. Buzz, as they called him, was a Navy Corpsman who had earned their respect by keeping them alive during combat operations.

Upon speaking with them, it immediately became apparent that their deep and profound respect for one another was cleverly hidden beneath and between barrages of ridicule and playful insults. Their keen, raw sense of humor had been honed by the stress of their service while simultaneously creating a sense of pride in being able to handle the highest of challenges. Their days in Iraq began with a drive past a sign dangling on the blast wall which read "Complacency Kills." If any one of them complained about minor inconveniences, made excuses, or reported grandiose claims, the others were quick to challenge the statement until the conversation exploded with laughter, accusation, and counter-arguments about the truth of the matter. In short, these Marines were smart, hilarious, proud men who had committed their lives to service and were immensely charismatic.

Nick enlisted in the Marine Corps twice in order to deploy to combat. He couldn't stomach the idea of completing his service in the United States Marine Corps without a combat deployment when Marines were fighting and dying in battle against an enemy whose tactics included attacking defenseless civilians. Matt served two combat tours and provided strength of leadership when other leaders were prone to hesitation, a flaw that endangered the lives of Marines. Nick remembered how an improvised explosive device (IED) detonated near him. I listened to him describe how "the horizon buckled." While everyone was still seeking to recover from the blast and regain their senses, Matt had already identified the person who detonated the IED and was leading a Marine reaction force toward him.

Buzz, who recognized the immense importance of earning the trust of the Marines he served with as a Navy Corpsman, actually led Marine patrols. He was committed to "leading from the front" and refused to ask anyone to do anything in combat that he wouldn't do himself. Buzz was a "dirt sailor," meaning he was a corpsman who preferred to be on the ground with Marines in combat rather than tucked away in the safety of a medical clinic. In order to deploy with Nick and Matt, Buzz repeatedly informed his leadership that, although they were requesting him to remain behind an array of different desks in the United States for the completion of various naval duties, there was "no way in hell" his Marines were deploying without him.

Buzz's commitment to ensuring his Marines were prepared to render medical aid, regardless of whether he was present, injured, or dead, paid off when an IED detonated beneath one of their five-ton vehicles near Ramadi. A Marine suffered a traumatic amputation, but as Buzz rushed to render aid to the Marine, he found lower enlisted Marines on scene had already applied tourniquets to the injured Marine while under small arms fire. The advanced training he'd given his Marines to ensure they could render medical aid effectively on the battlefield saved the life of one of their own.

Nick, Matt, and Buzz survived their military service and returned home to the United States. Buzz was the second-to-last person to get on the plane back; the last was the Battalion Commander. Upon returning home, and engrained with Marine Corps leadership principles, they confronted the reality that they needed new challenges and new missions to invest themselves in, both to make the world a better place and help them transition successfully into civilian life. So they focused on what they had always done: they served others.

Nick focused on service in the field of mental health. He became a Qualified Mental Health Associate and was a director of business for an outpatient mental health agency. He co-authored the book *Mental Health Emergencies: A Guide to Recognizing and Handling Mental Health Crises.* As he experienced the complex challenges associated with the mental healthcare system in the United States, Nick became committed to creating effective services that meet the needs of those facing the challenges associated with mental illness, ending stigmas associated with mental illness, and investing in the creation of innovative programs centered on mental health.

Matt served as a Police Officer, Licensed Social Worker, and Transition Care Manager for the Department of Veteran Affairs. He helped manage a caseload of more than 300 veterans, provided education and support services, and developed innovative outreach programs to engage the veteran population. Matt also worked for a non-profit organization that provided drug and alcohol programming for those who were incarcerated. Just as he had immersed himself in the duties and responsibilities of helping lead his Marines into being their very best in the most threatening, bleak and chaotic circumstances, he began to immerse himself in systems and programs designed to help service members and veterans cope with the effects of trauma and stress. His new focus is leading others through the transition from military service into success, health, and safety in the civilian world.

Buzz also began serving service members and veterans as a Transition and Care Management Patient Advocate at the Department of Veterans Affairs. He sought out military service members and veterans in need of services wherever he could find them. He didn't care where they were; Buzz met with them in inner city housing projects, apartments, houses, homeless shelters, under bridges, and in jails. After sitting down with one veteran whom physicians and psychiatrists were concerned about, Buzz and his partner were able to help stabilize the veteran and get him to return to the VA to connect him with services. It wasn't until after they'd gained the veteran's trust that they'd realized the muzzle of a loaded handgun had been pointed at them under the table the entire time they'd talked. It wasn't until the veteran realized that Buzz only had genuine intentions of wanting to help that the conversation could move forward. Buzz's commitment to selflessly serving veterans and his ability to gain the trust of men who've survived combat operations has not only saved the lives of service members, it has also saved his own.

As Nick, Matt, and Buzz navigated their home country's bureaucratic and often frustrating systems and agencies, they experienced their own challenges. But they knew to focus on their own personal development; as Matt said, "One thing I've learned in all my professional years is that you can't help someone else unless you've already helped yourself." They vented, brainstormed, confessed, raged, affirmed, and encouraged each other as they shared their personal, professional, and transitional challenges. After experiencing the healing power of self-care and mental health, Nick wanted to help those who may have had similar experiences to his own. Matt and Buzz also realized the power of what their collective insights, experiences, and knowledge had to offer to people who were facing challenges, regardless of whether or not they ever served in any military capacity.

Their discussions began to revolve around how they could help create the finest society possible for themselves and those they served. It was then that they discovered the Greek philosophers' Four Cardinal Virtues and began to realize the immense power these concepts held in their daily reflections and interactions. As they saw how these concepts positively affected them throughout their lives and the lives of those they served, their closest friends and loved ones also noticed the positive and appealing changes within them.

They realized that to create a field manual, one which blends their experiences with the four Cardinal Virtues, would be an offering that could potentially empower people to make sound and timely decisions when necessary, advance in the pursuit of their highest potential, instill the ability to remain calm under stress, become comfortable with the discomfort of positive growth, increase their stability and longevity, save marriages, and even prevent suicides.

This book is Nick, Matt, and Buzz's offering to you, but it doesn't come without strings attached. It is an offering that demands an action from you, the reader. Because you are important and you have value, it asks you to recognize the countless sacrifices that have been made in your honor. No matter who you are or where you are, there are men and women right now on battlefields in places you've never heard of, and never will, who are fighting and dying that you may make the most of every moment of your life. It asks you to drink deep the daily freedoms, securities, and pleasures you experience while developing increased courage, prudence, temperance, and justice so that you may sustain your brilliance. Nick, Matt, and Buzz and their friends have offered everything, sometimes resulting in severe injury, and sometimes even death, in order to give this gift to you. Don't waste that gift. Be the best possible you for the most possible time. Give them the gift of knowing that everything they sweat, bled, and fought for was worth it.

—**BEN BIDDICK,** co-author of *Get Up: The Art of Perseverance*, host of the Get Up Nation Podcast, U.S. Army veteran

Preface

by Stewart Smith, USN (SEAL)

WHEN IT COMES to debating which of the important virtues a warrior *must* have in order to be an optimal performer and a worthy citizen, the question is often asked: "Which is the most important to the warrior citizen?"

And throughout the ages, wise people have given their opinion on this matter. Socrates proposed four cardinal virtues—prudence, justice, temperance, and fortitude—naming temperance as the most important. Plato echoed his teacher's sentiment, identifying four cardinal virtues of his own: wisdom, bravery, temperance, and justice.

The list of virtues presented by the authors of this book—Nick Benas, Matt Bloom, and Buzz Bryan, tactical professionals all—leads with discipline.

Coming from a tactical profession myself—those being military, police, firefighters/EMTs—many will agree that discipline is the virtue that holds *all* other virtues together. When the days get long and turn into night, members of the tactical professions have to rely on their discipline to get the job done. Being a virtuous person—someone who is reliable, truthful, courageous, compassionate, humble, and disciplined—requires a "habit of the mind," as Cicero says.

The authors of this book have demonstrated how our present military virtues and core values have developed from the ancient writings and been modernized for today's warrior. They show why discipline is required for a person to show temperance; how with discipline it is easier to develop the other virtues needed from a warrior.

The virtues used to create the *The Warrior's Book of Virtues* are battle-tested from millennia of debate and discussion by the brightest minds and most successful warriors and leaders the world has ever seen. *The Warrior's Book of Virtues* takes these timeless classics and describes their evolution into today's society perfectly, in a way that is easy to read and understand for the citizen, the warrior, and the tactical professional population.

Above all, discipline and courage outweigh any other virtues, as without these, we would be unable to address and improve on the many virtues we hold as benefitting ourselves, our society and our world.

—STEWART "STEW" SMITH, USN (SEAL)

Introduction

"It is one thing to study war and another to live the warrior's life."

—TELAMON OF ARCADIA, MERCENARY, FIFTH CENTURY, B.C.

VIRTUE, BY DEFINITION, is the behavior or personality traits of an individual or group of people that exhibit a high standard of values and principles. In a more general sense, virtue means doing the right thing at the right time.

Virtue is the sum total of those character traits which we hold in the highest esteem: traits such as integrity, dignity, decency, courage and respectability. Some would argue these traits are culturally dependent; others, such as the Greek philosophers, credit each individual with the responsibility for their own personal development. (Of course, if the philosophers of that time felt they could help an individual along by personally taking someone under their wing, all the better; actively seeking out those who can help you better yourself is a virtue all its own).

Virtues and the traits of strong character are time-tested, with a proven track record in the making of great leaders and productive, altruistic societies. Yet the concept of virtue has become a pejorative in today's society. We denigrate and undermine the true meaning and value of virtue with hyperbolic, almost spiteful phrases like "*paragon of virtue.*" Take another phrase which has recently crept into the vernacular: "*virtue signaling,*" a term which implies the person in question is acting virtuous not out of any desire to better themselves or their world, but for the sake of gaining the attention and admiration of those around them. We belittle the true meaning of virtue through the words we use, and instill in our culture the idea that humans are inherently incapable of acting self-lessly, or in a virtuous manner. In its place has been a false sense of entitlement, instant and virtual gratification, excessive attachments to and destructive use of social media, disregard for traditional authority figures, and an assumed respect that is altogether unearned.

It's true: no one exhibits the qualities of virtue at all times. The reality of human error won't allow it. The outcome of any situation depends on a host of variables. Sometimes you have to prioritize individual safety, or the collective safety of those around you to complete an assignment. Other times, there are too many people in charge with too-varied opinions, or too few people in charge with no opinions; as a consequence, virtuous behavior falls to the wayside.

Human frailty and error won't allow for virtuous behavior 100% of the time. But if we consider the virtues of kindness and forgiveness, we recognize that no human being deserves the kind of pressure that comes with trying to be 100% virtuous every minute of every day.

That is why we are left, at the end of the day, with the ability to choose our attitude, to decide the best course for our efforts. We can make soulful considerations of conscience and commit to making better decisions, to do our best with the tools we can access within ourselves.

And that's why we're here. *The Warrior's Book of Virtues* was created with you, the reader, in mind, because building the lifestyle you desire requires you to be at your best. Both war and civilian life can be downright brutal, or they can be downright beautiful; the choice is yours. As Lieutenant General Victor Krulak, USMC (Ret.), said, "Everything in war is very simple, but the simplest thing is difficult. The difficulties accumulate and end by producing a kind of friction that is inconceivable unless one has experienced war."

The Warrior's Book of Virtues seeks to return virtue to the forefront, restoring time-honored values like honesty, integrity and perseverance, courage and temperance (self-restraint). Conceptualized and written by United States Marine Corps veterans, *The Warrior's Book of Virtues* is a discussion—not a sermon—on how to develop and embrace the skills of self-respect, respect for others and self-discipline. Working from a foundation of Plato's Four Cardinal Virtues—Prudence, Fortitude, Temperance and Justice—we'll explore how best to consistently live these virtues and thrive in our daily lives in easy, practical ways★.

No one's going to get it right all the time. That's not reality, and that's not what this book is about. It's about the deliberate, conscientious pursuit and eventual achievement of greatness, and the rejection of mediocrity and ambivalence. Life is an evolving, ever-changing and fluid process; it takes time to better ourselves, and our pursuit

---

★   *The authors have chosen to embrace Plato and his virtues in both their personal and professional lives because Plato was a warrior, one who motivated great men and put Socrates' teachings into action.*

of greatness must continue until the day that we leave this world behind. It's about the journey to becoming the best version of yourself and doing right by the person to either side of you. It's about discovery and fine-tuning the gifts and talents you've been given, overpowering fear, and opening yourself up to the endless possibilities that come with being a lifelong learner, while embracing the freedom and happiness you were meant to enjoy, for the sake of yourself and the people you love.

Life can seem like a wild ride on a broken Ferris wheel, seemingly out of our control. We get stuck at the top, the Ferris wheel not moving, or we get stuck in continuous motion, where the wheel won't stop, and we're stuck going around repeatedly, confined and feeling trapped. The ride finally stops on the ground, and we're left looking for mommy and daddy on the other side of the gate, with a seatbelt that won't unlock.

Your current world might be holding you back and controlling how you operate. In order for you to change the way you operate, you must equip yourself with the right tools and training for the highest order of discipline and virtue. Warriors affirm a high standard of values in order to live happy, healthy, financially stable, flourishing, successful lives.

If you're a civilian with no familiarity with military life, we understand if you struggle at times to relate with the experiences related in this book. All we ask is that you read with an open mind, let go of any attachment you may have to offensive words and labels, put aside politically charged opinions and biases, and treat *The Warrior's Book of Virtues* as your personal lifestyle field manual.

Finally, if you take nothing else from this manual, remember this: warriors lead, and lead with virtue. Warriors don't quit; they utilize courage and skill, they fight when necessary, and they don't give up.

How to read this book: This lifestyle field manual seeks to aid and equip you with the characteristics of a warrior of virtue. To this end, we make use of the following terminology at the end of each chapter:

ⓧ THE ENEMY. These are the obstacles that stand in the way of enjoying a virtue's benefits. They are the warning signs of a life lived without virtue, balance or order. They are your problem areas to identify, target and defeat.

⑨ 9-LINE REPORT. This is your plan of action. Based on nine stages of assessment, identification and resolution, this is how a warrior determines the best path forward to removing the enemy.

Ⓥ SIT-REPS. Short for Situation Reports, these appear at the end of each chapter and outline the key points to take away on each warrior virtue. They also include general guidance on how to better align your life with the ideals set forward in each chapter, to prepare you to adapt and overcome anything that stands between you and your best self.

1

DISCIPLINE

"I desire only to know the truth, and to love as well as I can, and, to the utmost of my power, I exhort all other men to do the same. I exhort you also to take part in the great combat, which is the combat of life, and greater than every other earthly conflict."
    —SOCRATES

"The pain of discipline is nothing like the pain of regret."
    —UNITED STATES MARINE CORPS

L ACK OF DISCIPLINE is a common problem we all must face, as individuals and as a society. The virtue of discipline has all but vanished from our households, often through no fault of our own. The standard family structure continues to evolve; large numbers of families are single-parent households, or live far away from extended family, which places limits on the time and incredible energy it takes to impart optimal moral training. The various circumstances of daily life further complicate matters: as more parents work longer hours to pay the rent, pay the mortgage or put food on the table, children are left more and more to their own devices (digital or otherwise) and want for the sort of strong, ordered upbringing they need to grow up well-adjusted and productive.

At one time, our society embraced the value of discipline. Whether it was learning to play a musical instrument, exercising, getting involved in organized sports, studying, or academic test-taking, we knew that meeting challenges head on and remaining committed to excellence was the standard to which we would all be held.

Fast forward to present day, and you may be wondering where all that discipline went! A lack of discipline and subsequent bad decisions have evolved into a culture plagued with unhealthy relationships, excessive college debt, and useless (or unused) degrees; we find it increasingly difficult to apply ourselves to our careers, or else we are unemployed, or have high anxiety and stress.

The good news is, even though discipline may have lied dormant within you for a number of years, you can still get back to that place. Socrates, the quintessential Greek philosopher, once said, "What makes a young man virtuous? Avoiding excess in anything. Poverty is a shortcut to self-control." You *can* go on to joyfully embrace a disciplined and virtuous life. With the aid of this lifestyle field manual, and the life experiences we've presented here—unapologetic and undisguised—we hope you will glean some insights to help you better yourself.

With proper application and practice, you can learn to embrace the virtues presented in the following pages. By doing so, you can work to dissolve even the most serious predicaments you find yourself in, as the barriers standing in your way evaporate.

And it all starts with discipline.

DISCIPLINE IN THE MARINES

Discipline—with a capital D—is the bedrock of the Marines. The Marine Corps defines discipline as the "willful obedience to all orders, respect for authority, self-reliance, and teamwork." Instruction in the art of discipline, considered a priceless tool by the ancient philosophers, imparts virtuous and moral training to help individuals make well-founded decisions and correct misbehavior, both in themselves and in others. The Marines understand that discipline is critical in the formation of the finest soldiers, sailors, and airmen, as well as some the finest, most productive citizens of any society or country.

Marines have a pattern they follow in order to succeed and win battles. Everything they do in their training and during exhaustive rehearsals is intentional and goal-oriented. Consistency, order and routine in turn creates discipline. The Marines perspective embeds a task-oriented, "take ownership" mentality that translates to winning in every aspect of life. It's hard to hit a target when you don't know what you're aiming at, right? Marines—warriors—don't have that problem: their target is always victory in battle; their aim is to live and live just on the other side of hard work and discipline.

The takeaway? In order to be successful, you need to know what your mission is. In order to succeed in your mission, it's critical that you master discipline in your approach.

Epictetus, the great Greek Stoic philosopher, knew this well. He held that individuals must be taught concepts of rigorous discipline in order to acceptably behave in society. Nobody wants to be around an asshole, but rarely do we do anything to address the difficult people in our midst other than to label the culprit. Epictetus knew that people *needed* to be held responsible for their own actions. There are so many external factors that are beyond our control, but things like our attitude, our behavior, and our affinity to self-discipline aren't among them. We control the sort of person we are, regardless of any obstacles. The Marines know it best: in order to live a successful life, you must adapt and overcome.

BEFORE BENAS TURNED *in every night at Parris Island (the Marine boot camp for those growing up and enlisting east of the Mississippi river), he found himself conducting the same disciplined ritual every night. He and eighty other recruits in his squad bay would sound off in unison from their place of attention, in front of their dated, nostalgic pre-Vietnam racks.*

Benas and his fellow recruits would roar with such intensity that the glass portholes of the squad bay would rattle. The drill instructor on duty would yell, "READY!" The recruits would respond with an explosive, ear-splitting, "SIR, ARE ALL THESE RECRUITS' RIFLES, FOOT LOCKERS, SEABAGS ALL SECURE? SIR, ARE ALL THESE RECRUITS' RIFLES ON SAFE, SIR?"

A long pause followed. All the while, the recruits remained stock still, at attention. Unbearable anticipation ebbed and flowed silently through the room, building behind the drill instructor's question. He would slowly move down the centerline of the squad bay, his biceps popping from his service Charlies short-sleeved khaki uniform, eyeballing recruits underneath his Smokey the Bear campaign cover. Finally, his response: "CHECK 'EM!"

The recruits in their short PT shorts and undershirts, feet wrapped in flimsy flip flops, would start screaming as one unit and swiftly sweep the combination padlocks on their footlockers, sea bags, and rifles, making a counter-clockwise rotation around their racks. They answered again, in unison: "DISCIPLINE, D-I-S-C-I-P-L-I-N-E, DISCIPLINE IS THE WILLFUL OBEDIENCE TO ALL ORDERS, RESPECT FOR AUTHORITY, SELF-RELIANCE AND TEAMWORK, SIR!"

In a matter of seconds, all while reciting this exceptionally effective mantra, the padlocks are checked and secured on the recruits' foot lockers, sea bags and rifles; the rifles are slung and secured on the rack, the weapons' safety mechanisms secured. Recruits were back in line in short order, in the center of their squad bay, only to find themselves following another set of commands: instructions to mount their rack, and then—lights out. Recruits on night fire watch patrolled every hour, on the hour, in the dark, a red lens over their moonbeam flashlight, tugging on the locks for their security checks. God forbid a safety lock on any rifle came loose when a DI tugged on it—it meant game over for Benas and his fellow recruits.

That discipline, which began in that Marine garrison, carried over to the deserts of Iraq. Benas, Bloom and Buzz carried M16-A2s and 9mm Beretta pistols; the weapons stayed on their person at all times and never left their side. The simple, repetitive and intentional exercises of accountability and habitual checking, double-checking, and triple-checking gear and weapons became more than habit. It was their work ethic: they slept with their gear and weapons, never more than arm's length away, if not slung or secured on the body. The boot camp locks were no longer needed; these Marines and the tools of their trade were no longer separate and distinct, but had been married together to become one unit, a process begun in their early days as fresh recruits. Repetitive tasks turned into a capacity for attention to detail, which evolved into life-saving techniques.

Everything learned during boot camp had a higher purpose. Just like any disciplined activity in life, attention to detail creates a greater awareness of the task at hand and allows you to adjust accordingly. This capacity is not restricted to the repeated behavior; it can transfer successfully to all other areas of your life. Discipline has a domino effect; mastering discipline means you learn faster, learn better. You retain more, and by stacking up new experiences and opportunities on top of existing discipline, you will achieve ultimate success—even when the chaos starts.

OBEDIENCE IN THE MARINES

As the previous episode shows, respect for authority and obedience to orders are drilled into the hearts, minds and souls of every Marine recruit from the minute they arrive at boot camp. The 243-year-old system, designed by the United States Marine Corps, is structured to turn recruits into better people and save lives when it counts. For Marines, discipline is the foundation of being a decent and productive citizen.

Without discipline, there can be no real relationship with others. The virtues of faithfulness, trustworthiness and integrity can only be honed over time. These are values born of early training, and discipline serves as the catalyst for these virtues' development. Practiced consistency leads to consistent practice, even when no one's looking—that is the warrior's mentality.

But there is more to discipline than self-discipline—especially in the Marines.

BLOOM RECALLS THE first time he was disciplined at boot camp. It was about three weeks into the 13-week training period, early June 1999—around noon chow time.

Going to chow in boot camp is not like going to a restaurant or a sit-down diner. It's regimented, planned and precise. A recruit was never empty-handed while moving about Parris Island between training evolutions; even in the 100-degree heat of South Carolina and while wearing full camouflage utilities, Bloom and his unit marched with weapons, load-bearing vests and a ditty bag (a small duffel bag) for each individual.

They marched together, moving as one unit. The drill instructors counted down and gave the commands: "Ground your gear. Move!" They would count down: "20, 19, 18…10…7…3, 2, 1." At this point, Bloom and his unit returned to the position of attention and awaited further instruction.

Bloom was moving slow that day. The exercise was to remove the load-bearing vest and stow it in the ditty bag. This was a timed exercise, with a time limit; Bloom did not finish in time. The results were: 1) Bloom jumped ahead and was already planning redemption on the next go-round; and 2) he missed the command to take one full canteen of water into the hall for noon chow time.

He made it into the chow hall, and the most welcome relief of air conditioning and solid food. It is customary for drill instructors to leave the recruits alone during chow time, so it came as a surprise to Bloom—sitting on the end of a row of tables in the proper eating position, feet at a 45-degree angle, back straight, non-feeding hand placed on the knee, bringing food to his mouth—when out of nowhere, he felt the presence of the heavy disciplinarian drill instructor. The DI bent over, his campaign cover resting on the side of Bloom's head—the only thing keeping *him from getting closer—and whispered in a slow, threatening growl, "Where the f#%@ is your canteen?"*

Before Bloom could respond with so much as the traditional preface of, "Sir, this recruit…" the drill instructor's whisper had exploded into a deafening roar. "Why the f#%@ don't you have a canteen with you?! Did you not hear MY COMMAND?! Are you gaffing me off?! What the f#%@ am I to tell your mother when you die of F#%@ING HEAT STROKE because you didn't pay attention to commands and bring a canteen with you?! Ah, you NASTY F#%@ING THING, GET THE F#%@ OUT of the chow hall!"

And just like that, Bloom blasted out of the chow hall, as did the entire platoon.

Bloom and his unit had a hell of a laugh about the whole thing weeks later, when they revisited the story. All the same, he never forgot a canteen again. The moral, according to Bloom? He didn't die, and he wasn't abused; he learned. And so did the rest of the platoon.

In today's society, it's often frowned upon to punish the group for the fault of the individual. But Marine Corps training teaches that the group is only as strong as its weakest link. Instead of seeing this as injustice, they consider it a motivator and an opportunity for the entire group to improve and master a critical set of skills that, in turn, contributes to the group's survival in the field.

The takeaway? A failure of discipline in one area of your life is not "made up for" by discipline in other areas. Your life, with all its different parts, must act as a unit, and is only as strong as its weakest link. The development of complete discipline, in all areas, results in improved performance and satisfactory task completion. This leads to positive change and a direct path to success.

THE VALUE OF their Marines training came into play one day in 2004. It was Buzz's first day of combat; he and his unit had been restlessly waiting for this and they were ready. They were positioned at Checkpoint 84, the staging area just outside the city of Fallujah in Iraq. Buzz was standing next to his Humvee out in the open air, ready and waiting. He had painstakingly made himself a real cup of coffee (or as real as it could be, given the circumstances) using all creative coffee-making means at his disposal. Every step in the process meant something; it had almost been a religious experience. No fast, easy tricks; just imaginative industriousness in full armor. He had his politically incorrect coffee cup, long-standing Sanka instant coffee, and the MREs (Meals Ready to Eat) container to heat the water.

Suddenly, chaos ensued. The unit is taking fire. Buzz wasn't sure from what direction, or who's shooting, but he jumped up, gripping the coffee in his hand. He thought to himself, 'I'm not dropping this damn cup of coffee.' For whatever reason his reflexes weren't going to let him put the full cup down.

Someone yelled at him, "C'mon! We gotta go!" Buzz hit the ground, the coffee went flying, now just another part of the chaos. A split second later, Buzz is back to his senses. He's a senior leader, they're taking fire, rounds are going everywhere, no one knows from what direction, or whether it's the good guys or the bad guys. No one knows a goddamn thing.

And now there's no goddamn coffee.

Buzz is annoyed and on full alert. There's smoke, disorder, confusion, dust; it's just loud chaos. The whole event is two parts horror movie to one part short comedy sketch.

Buzz laughs heartily now as he remembers the coffee chaos. Despite his irritation at his lost cup, he was willing to expose himself while taking fire to make sure his Marines were all present and accounted for. There was no thinking it through (after the coffee was declared a lost cause). Just doing—just taking immediate and effective action.

Buzz was awarded the Navy and Marine Corps Commendation Medal with Combat Distinguishing Device on August 26, 2005, for the work he did that day.

This story illustrates that even chaos can serve as a random means to a beneficial end. There's a parallel here to the chaos we experience in everyday life—obviously not to the intense level of battle in a war zone—but there's a comfort that comes from having the opportunity to demonstrate the virtues of courage and fortitude. There's a clear benefit to knowing with confidence that, when push comes to shove, you can remain clearheaded and disciplined, that you can work effectively and cohesively for a positive resolution for all. In a war skirmish or in a life skirmish, these glimpses of virtue shine all the brighter, bringing with them opportunities to use skills and a finely-tuned mind to dive into the deep end of sudden chaos without hesitation. Because you have a job to do, and you're going to do it—coffee or no coffee.

WILLFUL OBEDIENCE

What does willful obedience look like? It means following orders or rules with intention; in other words, being fully aware as to *why* you're following an order or rule and still keeping any emotional influence or opinions at bay. Being willful means that you are able to submit deliberately, with full recognition of why you are doing so and what that decision means.

Willful obedience goes hand in hand with a respect for authority. Respecting the individuals in power, along with those entrusted to make decisions on behalf of the unit, group, or organization, for the benefit of all and to secure the best possible outcome—whether you agree with those decisions or not—is essential for any kind of organized success.

Rules, laws, customs, and cultural expectations are meant to enforce harmonious living, as well as influence a group's collective behavior. Following these rules demonstrates a respect for yourself as well as a respect for others, which is just as critical for success. When a group is united by mutual respect, the individual is able to focus on their goals and solve problems, knowing that everyone else on the team is doing the same—just like Marine recruits learning to operate in a cohesive manner to accomplish a common aim.

DISCIPLINE EXERCISE

Are you in control of your own thoughts and emotions? Before you can order your external world take an inventory of your internal world. Does your mind replay thoughts about the past or race to sort through the future? Do your thoughts obey your mind? Does your body respect your own inner authority to calm itself when you are stressed? Can you connect to your own inner resources in a time of stress without depending on other people to meet your emotional needs? Can you maintain your composure when you connect and collaborate with other people?

It is often difficult to maintain discipline in times of stress. Practicing self-discipline before things are stressful can make it easier to automatically access your skills when you need them in times of stress.

Start by taking control of your own breath. This is the one part of our body's stress response we can control. When we are stressed we tend to breathe fast and shallow. When we are calm and relaxed we breathe slow and deep. Can you slow your own breath when you want to? Just notice. What is your breath like right now? Is it fast and shallow or is it slow and relaxed? Try counting slowly to 4 as you breathe in. One, two, three, four... Pause and notice what you feel in your body. Now slowly count to four again and breathe out all the way. Pause again and notice. What do you feel in your body?

Different people experience different things when they start a breathing practice for the first time. It is normal for an undisciplined mind to resist structure at first. Be patient with yourself and keep practicing.

It's easy to get distracted and it's easy to be lazy. This is universal; it applies to everyone. Sometimes you have to do stuff you don't want to do. Sometimes you have to get out of bed in the morning and go to a job you despise. But the danger of settling for less than you are capable of is the risk of becoming directionless. Implementing discipline will help you fight through lazy periods; acting responsibly, even when it's difficult, will help you grow, and to live the life you desire. Recognize that your low periods are temporary, and that it is within your power to make changes. Don't settle. Take a self-inventory: are you living the way *you* want to live? Are you living your life for others; to impress your parents; to appease your boss?

None of these scenarios are anything new, but it is time for reveille. It is time to start living with discipline and virtue. You are responsible for the decisions you make and the actions you take, and ultimately for this one life you've been gifted. It's okay to do your best with yourself, for yourself. No one can tell you not to put the work in to make yourself the best version of yourself you can be.

DISCIPLINE: THE ENEMY

To defeat your enemy, you first have to know your enemy. When there is a lack of discipline, the following warning signs appear:

- ⊗ **Self-absorbed perception**. Everything starts to attack you, your attention and your precious time.

- ⊗ **Weak character**. Negativity, selfishness (the inverse of self-discipline), laziness, sloth-like behavior, arrogance, harsh and myopic judgement of others.

- ⊗ **Poor treatment of people**. Unproductive criticism of others, mistreatment of others; failing to treat others as you would like to be treated.

- ⊗ **Poor listening skills**. Over-talking others, inter-rupting in conversation; missing or ignoring others' body language.

- ⊗ **Lack of personal growth**. Stopping your lifelong learning and accepting ignorance; giving up on self and others.

- ⊗ **Anxiousness**. Fear about any given situation; looking to the future with concerns for the unknown.

- ⊗ **Long-term stress**. Lacking discipline in your day-to-day life.

- ⊗ **Compounding daily life and work problems**. This shows an inability to adapt to your present envi-ronment; taking work home with you, obsessing over the past only holds you back.

- **(X) Being your worst by acting badly** and submitting to your weaknesses as a form of addiction. Denial; refusing to address personal problems.

- **(X) Lack of self-restraint**. Engaging in self-destructive bodily pleasures. Extreme drugging, sex, plucking, cutting, excessive masturbation, self-harm, and mutilation.

- **(X) Poor health**. Ignoring morbid obesity, bulimia or anorexia; neglecting nutrition and exercise; ignoring medical and professional advice or input; letting prescriptions lapse.

- **(X) Financial illiteracy**. Making poor financial decisions, being broke, spending more than you make, and placing yourself in crushing debt.

- **(X) Broken relationships**. Verbal, emotional or physical abuse; staying with an abusive partner.

- **(X) Social instability**. Being afraid to speak your mind and contribute to social discourse

- **(X) Being unsuccessful in your job due to lack of effort.** Jumping from dead end job to dead end job; inability to keep a job.

- **(X) Lack of intellectual virtues**. Lack of curiosity, poor learning environment; inability to make time for personal exploration and development.

- **(X) Explosive behavior**. Things like road rage leading to physical harm, premature death or incarceration/ jail time.

- **(X) Bad-mouthing others**. Gossiping; cyber-bullying.

Ⓧ Obsessing over other people's ideas or suggestions. Putting too much stock in someone else's opinion, including friends and family. Incapability or refusal to make adult decisions.

DISCIPLINE: 9-LINE REPORT

We've identified the enemy. What's our plan of action?

1 **Check-in:** Take an honest assessment of who and where you are in your life at this moment. What kind of person are you? If you can't be honest with yourself, then you're not ready to make changes.

2 **Identify the issues:** Why am I undisciplined? Don't make excuses—make sound judgements. Is my current life set up for success, or am I just existing?

3 **Prioritize:** Start a journal or a blog. Brainstorm what you want in life, and visualize self-discipline succeeding for you. Implement discipline in a way that fits you. Don't cop out; you need to challenge yourself.

4 **Make a plan:** Visualize the next step. Make a plan for both your short-term and long-term goals. If you intend to complete all your tasks by the end of the day, that's great. But start by not hitting snooze on your morning alarm and making your bed. That's two goals met in two minutes. Stick to the plan, and hold yourself accountable.

5 **Set goals:** Immediate, short, and long; we touched on this briefly. Discipline is doing the small things, paying attention to detail when no one is looking, and living a life of commitment and integrity. Set goals and make a commitment to let your goals guide you.

6 **Commit:** The steps you have to take will not all be easy. You're going to fail, fall short, and get frustrated. But know this: that's what personal growth is. Growth can be painful and uncomfortable. Console yourself in the moment with this fact: you are learning, even if you can't see or feel it in the moment. Most of the time, we won't notice ourselves growing; it's too new, too uncomfortable. But you're becoming a better and more disciplined person because of your efforts. Stick to your plan, even when shit hits the fan. This is discipline—in all its glory.

7 Execute the plan: This isn't the time to stick your toes in the water to test the temperature. Dive in. Hesitation tends to snowball and causes a plan to fail before it can even begin.

8 Evaluate: Did you progress? Did you regress? Was your plan ineffective? Depending on what plan you are executing, take some time to reflect on what went well, what ended badly, and adjust your fire. We continually make adjustments, because life is a series of adjustments. If you nail your plan the first time and think you did a great job, you're either lying to yourself or failed to truly challenge yourself. There's always room for improvement. Roll your sleeves up, and do some real work.

9 Fire for effect: You have now built up some great life habits. Now, use them in all areas of your life. Make them a part of your work ethic and adjust your lifestyle accordingly. Avoid limiting your abilities. Becoming a warrior is a lifestyle commitment, not something you use temporarily to pass a test, land a date, or get a promotion. Use what you've developed, own it, and keep chasing the best version of you.

DISCIPLINE: SIT-REP

- ☑ **Make discipline a *habit* and an *application* in all things**. Doing so will provide you with freedom in your life. You must discipline your behaviors, daily desires and daily routines.

- ☑ **Face your fears**. Take immediate responsibility for yourself and your actions. Hold yourself accountable. If you mess up, acknowledge it and file it away. Tomorrow really is another day.

- ☑ **Put your phone down and turn your television off**. Evaluate your time spent on recreational activities with family and friends and decide whether this is the best use of your time.

- ☑ **Develop an operational plan**. Write out your daily intentions, short-term and long-term goals. Eliminate excuses. Recognize them instantly and eliminate them. Replace excuses with productive action.

- ☑ **Model yourself after those who are successful** in spaces you want to occupy and excel in. Surround yourself with people who lift you up and make you a better person; avoid those who tear you down.

- ☑ **Work your body out every day**. Our bodies were meant for movement. Evaluate your eating patterns and your nutrition and make necessary changes. Take sleep and nutrition seriously.

- ☑ **Develop your talents**. Identify and develop your passions. Eliminate self-absorbed and gratuitous behavior.

√ **Get up early**. Start your day at 0430 (yes, that's 4:30 AM) and go to bed early in the evening. Quality sleep will never be a concern when you live a structured lifestyle and fill it with actionable items. Keep charging ahead throughout the day, even when it gets uncomfortable. Take necessary breaks—even a nap if you need to—and finish the task you started. Allow yourself to push through the pain now and again.

√ **Remain faithful to yourself.** Take the time to get to know and trust the people who love you.

√ **Make sound decisions for the sake of your physical and mental well-being**. Focus on both your mental and physical health, as the two are inseparable. Having a strong body has tremendous positive effects on your overall health and sense of well-being. When you are well, you can take on even the most difficult tasks.

√ **Develop your own discipline systems** in order to create a sense of structure that works for you, and which you can take personal pride in. Having structure allows for disciplined behavior to be consistent throughout your life.

2

PRUDENCE

"What we plant in the soil of contemplation, we shall reap in the harvest of action."
   —Meister Eckhart, German theologian
   and mystic

THE ANCIENT GREEKS considered the virtue of prudence to be the framework for moral virtue. Often referred to as practical wisdom, prudence is the ability to govern and discipline oneself with reason; to show skill in one's use of resources, as well as the ability to make right decisions when called upon to do so.

PRUDENCE IN THE MARINES

Active duty Marines are often confronted with the most difficult, split-second "right" decisions a person will ever have to make. Someone's life might depend on them correctly assessing a situation and making the right call; or, the consequences of their decisions might impact their safety, and the safety of fellow Marines, military personnel and civilians. To see situational reality for what it is at that precise moment, with virtually no time to analyze or second-guess; to act dutifully, quickly and efficiently, even when it might mean taking a life or stacking a body—that's reality for a Marine. That is the world they are called to embrace.

NICK BENAS REMEMBERS vividly one experience in the desert that caused some of the people involved to second-guess their decisions.

One day, he and his unit were on patrol. Their assignment was to keep a section of Iraqi highway safe, to accurately identify and investigate any suspicious objects and activity, and to keep the highway free of debris. This meant physically patrolling the area, riding a Humvee, all senses on high alert, and surveilling the area repeatedly to get a feel for things—what's in its place and what's not. There were times when they'd secure the perimeter only to come 'round again and find potato sacks, trash and debris that were not there earlier.

So when something that was non-existent earlier was all of a sudden visible, it raised a red flag. They also knew the Mujahedin (enemy Muslim guerrilla fighters) would often heat the asphalt of the highway in random locations with diesel, remove the asphalt, plant Improvised Explosive Devices (IEDs) in the resulting gaps in the road, and then reseal the asphalt, very effectively hiding the device, which could be set off using a cell phone. The possibility of this happening was never far from their minds.

Benas and his squad were on patrol, approximately 100 yards out, when they counted (with binoculars) first one, then two bodies lying on their backs on the highway. Upon investigation, they determined the unclothed corpses were not the enemy, but that the Mujahedin had probably killed the men and stuffed their body orifices with explosives. The dead were later identified as Iraqi National Guardsmen.

The unit cordoned the area off, concluded the explosives were two 155 Howitzer rounds with a Nokia cell phone attached for a trigger, and waited several hours for the Explosive Ordnance Disposal (EOD) unit to arrive. The EOD finally showed up and, using a robot equipped with tank treads, camera and extending arms, placed a water charge to disable the IED. Afterwards, Benas and his unit were given the green light to dispose of the dead.

Keenly aware that their responsibility was to keep the highway free and clear of any debris—including but not limited to corpses stuffed with explosives—they stood around for a short time, talking disjointedly with no real plan for how to dispose of the bodies. The squad knew they had to finish what they started, that they were obligated to dispose properly of the bodies. So, weighing their limited options, they tied the corpses' ankles and arms using rope, placed them onto the narrow hood of their Humvee and drove them to the Iraqi National Guard compound.

As their Humvee approached the gate, Benas recalls seeing a group of men on the inside just standing around, showing no willingness to assist. The driver of the Humvee rolled the vehicle in, only for the unit to realize they had no gloves with which to move a bloody, dead body. Resisting the temptation to compare this unfortunate experience to a sick parody of a Three Stooges routine, the driver quickly took the situation into his own hands and made the executive decision to drive forward slowly, then abruptly brake. Repeating this process, he continued his improvised procedure until the bodies rolled off the Humvee hood, dropped to the ground in front of the vehicle, and immediately became the property of the Iraqi National Guard.

Effective, certainly; but those involved that day walked away with their consciences unsettled, bothered by the possibility they had treated the bodies with disrespect.

These warriors used what resources they had at their disposal to accomplish their task. They played the cards they'd been dealt, fulfilled their responsibilities, and can say without hesitation they followed orders.

Bottom line: they completed their job as assigned that day. They protected the living. They kept the road clear of debris, which was their charge.

Benas' job that day didn't end the way the unit intended. But we can't always control the situations we find ourselves in. The real question is, did they act with integrity? Did they think things through? Would it have made a difference if, had they been able to overcome the language barrier, they'd asked for assistance from those on the other side of the gate? Or would that have exposed the living to danger or disease? Were they better off getting the bodies out of their possession as fast as possible and getting the hell out of there?

Were their actions, from start to finish, ones of integrity—of virtue?

Prudence is making the right decision based on your current set of circumstances. Prudent thinking and acting influence how we behave, deliberate, and prioritize things every day. Someone who has mastered prudence can exercise it in all areas of their life. Prudent thinkers manage their lives with careful execution and self-restraint; they typically shop around for a car, rather than buying the first car on the used car lot. Using prudence in today's fast-paced, internet-driven and virtually-influenced society, where a gazillion choices are on the table at any given time, takes self-restraint, patience and discipline. But know this: when you master prudence, *how* you do something becomes how you do other things in life. Virtue, as we've said, is a domino chain; each area of life that you live virtuously positively affects every other area of your life.

As a warrior, implementing prudence is critical. You need to ensure your acts of bravery don't become acts of carelessness and, ultimately, weakness. You need to make sound decisions that will positively impact your life.

RESPONSIBILITY IN THE MARINES

To a Marine, every job is a responsibility—an opportunity to practice and personify efficiency, common sense and prudence to the best of their ability. The procedures endured in training, the refinement of human capability and honing of talent, lead to the creation of well-laid plans, executed using optimum performance which lead to successful missions when and where it counts most.

This perspective extends down to the smallest detail. For example, Marines are always on time. They show up on time (frequently early) and they are never late to their destination. It's even an unwritten rule to be at least 15 minutes early to a formation or work task. That means that if a Battalion Commander wants his Marines in formation at 0530 (5:30 am), those Marines are showing up at 0400 (4:00 am). And the directive keeps moving through the chain of command: the platoon leader shows up at 0415, the squad leaders arrive at 0430, and the fire team leaders make their appearance at 0445.

Even in those situations where the best-laid plans go awry, where prudent preparation fails to lead to the desired outcome, Marines remain composed and focused; they know that so long as they remain prudent and professional, there will be any number of opportunities to turn failure into success.

Secluded in a *beautiful oasis near the Al Asad air base in Iraq stands a makeshift training ground for the Iraqi police. Beside the handful of tents set aside for the recruits sits an abandoned school house, where dusty students' desks remain stuck in time, chalkboards affixed to walls still with Arabic writings and numbers etched on them. A broken seesaw and a rusted-out jungle-gym sit alone, seemingly decades old.*

Sandstorms are frequent here, but don't last very long; neither do the dust devils that pop up here and there. Russian-model Iraqi fighter planes, grounded and scattered about the area, are grim leftovers from the Persian Gulf War, half-dug into the ground and covered with camouflage netting, graffiti left on the exposed and aged aircraft still visible to the naked eye.

In 2004, Benas, Bloom and Buzz's unit was tasked with the responsibility of training the police recruits and exchanging custody with the previous coalition forces and civilian contractors after the initial invasion of Iraq. On one occasion, already geared up, prepped and ready to attack the day, Benas headed out on assignment. His task: to pick up another Marine and an Iraqi translator, turn around back to base to pick up the recruits, then turn around again and get them to the oasis training ground locale.

Benas had calculated the mission to be a 20–30-minute drive via paved highway, along some twisting and bumpy dirt roads, and through a metal scrap yard. However, he's running late because a Gunnery Sergeant added a last-minute check-in formation for the few Marines present. The staff non-commissioned officer in question usually acted in a more administrative role; this was an out-of-the-blue side show for the 4–6 Marines on site.

Benas was running behind schedule, driving a stick shift Hyundai bus, the Arabic translator and fellow Marine retrieved, on his way to his final destination. But as the bus approached the main gate at the base, a large explosion rippled through in front, behind, all around— the horizon abruptly buckled. As best Benas could determine, it had come from outside of the main gate.

He brought the bus to a stop just in front of the barrier and was met by a Military Police Officer who was stopping all traffic. It turned out that a VBIED (Vehicle-Borne Improvised Explosive Device) had detonated in front of them. Benas begged and pleaded to be let through the base gate so he could pick up his police recruits, but no luck.

The irony of the situation wasn't lost on him or his passengers: Marines are expected to be punctual, yet if they had been on time, chances were good they'd be among the dead. Benas had tried his best to be on time *that morning, but a series of unforeseen events slowed him down. The plan became an adaptive, revise-as-you-go with what you know situation. That was part of his training, as well: things change, you make adjustments.*

As Benas finally got through the main gate, he could see the brutal case-in-point: plans gone awry, turned askew, made real by the damage and the dead bodies of his recruits. And they were his recruits; at the end of the day, they were his responsibility, under his protection, now laying dead close to where they were smoking cigarettes and waiting to be picked up moments before.

We try our best to maintain order and structure in everything we do, but sometimes life has other plans. Universal human fault and frailty on the character spectrum force us to acknowledge that there are limits to how much control we can have over the things that happen to us. It doesn't mean we should expect to fail—it means we should cultivate the sort of mental toughness and foresight needed to roll with the punches as best we can, and keep moving forward.

PRACTICING FORGIVENESS

Holding onto negativity which stems from past life events you no longer have any say or control over takes a massive toll on our emotional, mental, physical, and spiritual health. Likewise, it requires a conscious decision to acknowledge that we have control over our own actions and our own attitudes in this life…and that's *it*.

When negative past experiences prevent you from moving forward in life, it not only wreaks havoc on your body; it takes over the driver's seat in your life, often leading to unhealthy relationships at home, work and school. This in turn impacts your productivity, health, wealth and ultimate success. We must find ways to accept responsibility for these feelings, perceptions and actions surrounding darkness from the past. When we stop being the victims of other people and start taking responsibility for ourselves, our actions and reactions, we gain an even greater sense of self-worth and confidence.

Being able to forgive yourself (and others) for stupid things you've done or witnessed in the past can be difficult. But doing so will help lessen the resentment, anger and hostility we tend to direct at people and events, both past and present. Thankfully, the act of forgiveness knows no timeline. Learning from the mistakes we've made is a difficult exercise in practicing prudence, temperance, justice and fortitude all in one. In order to resolve the guilt we all feel about mistakes we've made, one must make forgiveness a daily and deliberate practice. Consistency, whether through prayer, meditation, walking in nature, journaling, talking things out with a trusted friend, or some kind of conscious mindfulness practice, will lead to healing the frustration, anger, shame, contempt for others, hostility, and resentment attached to those memories.

PRUDENCE IN RELATIONSHIPS

Learning to forgive another person can lessen the impact their negative actions and attitudes have on us, but there are times when simply reducing their influence is not enough. It is a waste of time and energy—two of the most valuable resources we have—to involve ourselves with those who lack the desire or ambition to repair their relationships or correct their harmful behaviors.

For example: say your parent was (and still is) a non-functioning alcoholic while you were growing up, and is still destroying their job, their relationships and their bodies with a self-destructive over-consumption of alcohol. You've made your concerns known and done your best to offer assistance, love and support, but the situation refuses to change.

Though it may be hard to contemplate, there may come a time when the best thing you can do for your own well-being and your inviolable right to live your life free of toxic situations is to draw boundaries and prudently walk away.

This doesn't mean abandoning your loved one entirely; it means accepting the fact they may never change. Your parent might die sick and unhappy and there is very little you can do about it. There is a level of acceptance here, connected to yet distinct from the forgiveness of self. By taking action—by removing yourself from those environments that don't benefit you or which harm you—is acting prudently. You can't always fix a situation, but you can always do what is best at that moment, under those circumstances. That is what it means to be a prudent, responsible adult who takes ownership of their own well-being and happiness.

PRUDENCE EXERCISE

Behavior is often driven by our thoughts and emotions, and sometimes unconscious thoughts can lead to "unrighteous" behavior. We often are not aware of the ways we violate our own values until after we fail to exercise prudence.

When evaluating our behavior after the fact, we may find that we have acted wrongly, either for our own personal values or those of the society we live in. And while forgiveness is easy to understand, it is often difficult to practice. Before you begin your own forgiveness process, it can be helpful to take a moment to remind yourself you are human—humans make mistakes, and it is okay to learn from your past.

Take a deep breath. As you do, take an inventory of your personal history and try to notice any memories of times when you feel like you could have acted differently. Choose one memory to start with.

Notice any thoughts, emotions or body sensations that are connected to the memory you want to work with. Take another deep breath. Remind yourself that this memory happened in the past and that it is okay to let it stay in the past. In your mind, imagine playing out a movie of the memory. In the movie in your mind, watch yourself acting the way you wish you could have acted the first time. Notice what it feels like in your body to imagine doing things differently; whether it is helpful to imagine yourself acting according to your personal values in a similar future situation. Again, notice what it feels like in your body to imagine a future situation in which you exercise prudence.

End your movie with one last deep breath.

RECOVERY FROM TRAUMA

The impact that past traumas have on our present lives is very real and often difficult to overcome. The time it takes to recover is specific to the individual and is indeterminate. Sadly, some people never recover. That's why it is so critical for our recovery that we learn to forgive others and ourselves, no matter how minor or trivial the event.

However, we often aren't sure how or where to begin. Here's the first step: we must learn to recognize our anger, hostility, and resentment behaviors, and then work to identify what our triggers are for these behaviors. Developing and implementing the skill of awareness is the first step to recognizing when we are triggered—to recognizing the thoughts, emotions and actions associated with these triggers, and how best to take quick action to move destructive thoughts and painful, negative memories to the side.

Don't waste time or headspace feeling sorry for yourself. It offers no positive benefits, and you risk getting stuck, both physically and emotionally, if you allow what has happened to you to control you—or worse, control those who love and care for you.

It is both practical and prudent to admit when you've been wrong, to recognize that tragedy is a setback. Acknowledge what has happened, acknowledge your anger, hurt, and any other resentment behaviors, and work toward healing and recovery. Certainly reach out for help; go easy on yourself while you are processing things, and forgive yourself if you regress into negativity or anger. But if you can find the inner strength to deal with the crappy things that happen in life, rather than deny they ever happened, you'll emerge stronger than ever, just in time to live a happy life.

You also need to accept that what helps one person heal may not help the next. Some people find success with individual talk therapy with a professional therapist or counselor. Some folks find success with self-care strategies like prayer, meditation, journaling, yoga, Pilates, high intensity exercise, church activities, gaming, club sports, Tuesday bowling, Thursday golf, or support groups, along with the trusted support of friends and family.

There's no one "right" answer here, and there's no one 'right' way to heal from trauma, so respect the process. Draw on your courage, ask questions and seek answers. Avoid comparing yourself to others with similar experiences who seem to be doing better than you—or, if you tend to empathize, worse than you. This is one time in your life when you need to focus on yourself. This isn't a contest or a race. Find an advocate, if you are lucky enough to have that option. Use the tools at your disposal. Many communities offer financial assistance to low income populations and single parents. Understand this, for your sake and the sake of your loved ones: if we don't acknowledge what's going on and get help, we end up transmitting our inner darkness onto other people we care about instead of behaving courageously and doing the work to transform our lives and be happy.

Recognizing these moments as opportunity isn't easy. It takes a conscious decision, and it's your pursuit toward mindfulness. For great self-help strategies and mindfulness exercises, please refer to the Appendix on page 165.

PRUDENCE: THE ENEMY

To defeat your enemy, you first have to know your enemy. When there is a lack of prudence, the following warning signs appear:

- ⊗ **Decision-making based on bad habits and utter stupidity**. Preoccupation with self, fame and possessions. Going after something seen as attractive or valuable, to extremes.

- ⊗ **Hostile, belligerent or berating behavior**. Booming voice, profanity and aggressive bodily gestures; overuse of the middle finger. Exhibiting hostile traits and/or undue aggressiveness; overreacting toward trivial events; transferring blame to others, seeing the "wrong" in every situation.

- ⊗ **Irrational behavior**. Avoidance of vicious extremes or deficiencies. Inappropriate lack of trust in others; ignoring advice or input from people who genuinely care about you.

- ⊗ **Carelessness**. Deliberate disregard and apathy for cultural beliefs, morals, rules and laws of the environment and time you currently occupy. Neglect of property or self, family and/or pets.

- ⊗ **Oversensitivity**. Overreaction to constructive criticism. Inability to appreciate yourself or compliment other individuals; inability to receive compliments.

- ⊗ **Being argumentative**. Becoming immediately defensive on a regular basis. Using "I," "Me," or "My" when speaking to others.

ⓧ **Being financially illiterate**. Blowing off bills, overextending with credit cards to purchase material things and not paying it back; paying only the minimum payment due when you can afford to pay more; being a "shop-a-holic"; overextending with student loans.

ⓧ **Recklessness**. Ignoring speed limits, accelerating through red lights, leaving car and home doors unlocked, leaving keys in the ignition or infants/toddlers in the car.

ⓧ **Judging others unfairly**. Thinking that others are to blame for your actions or shortcomings.

ⓧ **Tardiness**. Inability to keep to a schedule, keep appointments or meet deadlines.

PRUDENCE: 9-LINE REPORT

We've identified the enemy. What's our plan of action?

1 **Check in:** What decision needs to be made? The content or size doesn't matter; only your responsibilities and resources.

2 **Identify:** What makes this decision or task unique? Nothing should just be "routine"; every situation has its own variables that need to be assessed and reassessed.

3 **Prioritize:** Determine which of the tasks in front of you is most important. Quickly think things through and visualize your tasks in order from more important to least important—and then act.

4 **Make a plan:** Go over the pros and cons of each side of the decision. Prudence, by definition, is the use of care and caution. So do it! Making a decision without a plan or information is like a disaster waiting to happen. Luck is not a guarantee, and it's not tangible; never base your life around luck.

5 **Set goals:** What do you want to achieve or gain from this decision? Take the time to look at your life's priorities and see how this moment aligns with them.

6 **Commit:** Be firm in your decision. Don't waver, even if you get dragged through the mud. You're not always going to come out on top or unscathed. What you thought was wise and correct may not always be the case. Either way, learning has occurred.

7 **Execute:** Being prudent doesn't necessarily mean taking all day to decide. This process can occur fairly quickly, especially if you're exercising proper discipline. Procrastination is the evil cousin to prudence. Don't get caught up in the process; make use of these steps and go!

8 **Evaluate:** Take stock after the dust settles. How accurate was my judgement? Was it on point? Did I identify all necessary areas, or did I miss something? Were my thoughts off base or in completely the wrong zip code? Pass or fail, make sure you take something from your experience.

9 **Fire for effect:** Regardless of the outcome, trust the process. Live, learn, repeat. Life will go on, with or without you; don't hold yourself back.

PRUDENCE: SIT-REP

- Ⓥ **Work on your physical, mental and spiritual well-being**. Exercise your body with weights. Leverage your body, incorporating cardio workouts, good nutrition, hydration and alternative exercises such as yoga, martial arts, hiking, biking, basketball, golf, etc. Exercise mental health with therapy work, mindfulness activities, meditation, self-help strategies, and professional supports.

- Ⓥ **Be prudent with your finances and work on becoming financially literate**. Spend less than you make. Live frugally, modestly and minimally. Turn the lights off when you leave the room and before you go to bed at night. Invest in financial literature and education (debt management, financial planning, budgeting, tax planning and preparation). Pay all your bills in advance or on time. Chip away and remove all debts.

- Ⓥ **Conduct a weekly summary of your purchases**. What time of the day do you make your purchases? When making purchases, do you find yourself alone or with someone else? Calculate your weekly total spent on each item. Do you notice any particular behaviors when you are spending the most? What changes can you start to make to reduce your spending habits/ behaviors?

- Ⓥ **Do not borrow money from friends and family members**. Likewise, do not lend money or resources to friends and family members. If you're a business owner, always pay yourself first, then your employees.

✓ **Reduce excess at home and work**. Strip yourself of personal effects and knick-knack dust collectors. If it doesn't make you happy or serve a function, give it to Goodwill.

✓ **Trim and slim down your activities**. Say no to that committee, fundraiser, speaking engagement or request for pet-sitting unless it feeds you or gives you a sense of joy. Reduce the amount of escapist activities you partake in (social media, video games and other mindless distractions)

✓ **Avoid confrontations**. They are a waste of time and energy. Learn and develop conflict resolution tactics and listening skills. Take control of your emotions. Study mindfulness practices. This will require discipline extending to your personal health such as fitness, nutrition and mindful practices.

✓ **Learn to give and receive constructive criticism and feedback from others**. It's always a good idea to ask if someone wants ideas first. Be respectful if they decline your offer. Always remember, the other person doesn't have to listen to you.

✓ **Stop making excuses**. Find a person in your life you trust who will tell you when you're making excuses and trust them. Even better, make a pact to hold each other accountable. Always respect and thank them when they have the courage to tell you the truth. Ultimately, it makes you better.

● **Identify problems in your life, accept them as teachable moments, learn from them and move away from them**. Start moving forward by taking action with good, sound decision-making that weighs all the pros and cons. Some people can dive in and take huge amounts of action with large quantities of productivity; others take baby steps. Both are correct. Find what works for you and stay with it. When you make a mistake, go back and review if you acted in prudence.

● **Manage your personal space.** This includes both at work and at home, as well as in your relationships with all the people in your life. Make decisions based on need, organization and efficiency.

3

TEMPERANCE

"Eat not to dullness; drink not to elevation."
—BENJAMIN FRANKLIN

TEMPERANCE IS THE act of self-discipline, self-restraint (*sôphrosune* in Greek), and moderation in all activities. Exercised properly, temperance brings us to a more mindful, more self-aware state—it can make warriors of us all.

Temperance is the ability to turn away from the temptations of temporary pleasure and immediate self-gratification. It is when you act as a warrior does, refraining from fruitless imbibing or pointless aggressive acts, and instead choosing to resolve challenges through forgiveness, nonviolence and diplomacy. This should be your way of life.

This is not to say that there will never come a time when you will have to make a decision, one which involves a very calculated and aggressive act of violence towards another human being, in order to save yourself and the people around you. This can be understood both literally, as is often the case on the battlefield, as well as figuratively: there may come a time when you have no choice but to say or do something that will hurt another person—mentally, emotionally, or socially, as well as physically—but which is necessary to protect you and the people who count on you.

Tempering your character weaknesses now, choosing to endure the struggle and uncomfortableness that comes with any positive personal change, should be your focus as you look to lead a successful and happy life. Make a commitment now to be a lifelong learner. If you aren't happy with the feelings that come of being an unsettled soul, then make a change. Don't be afraid to be happy. One of life's many truths is we rarely know the good we're truly capable of until we get fed up and take action. We often end up surprising ourselves, as well as others.

Temperance is also control over the threat of excess in our life. It means taking action with courage to manage chronic illness, for example, or an indulgent, self-destructive behavior like alcoholism. People who struggle with substance abuse problems make the decision to stop every day—it *can* be done. We are fortunate enough to live in a society with established programs to assist in things like out-patient care or addiction recovery, but in every case the individual has to commit to those treatment modalities and to a certain way of life. They must make use of their pre-existing discipline of mind to temper themselves, to remain clear and committed to what is required for a healthy lifestyle.

Temperance also means being humble, understanding the contributions of those around you, giving and receiving forgiveness, and exhibiting healthy levels of confidence and kindness. Truly, to master temperance is to become authentic.

Success in life brings with it an opportunity to choose humble confidence or obnoxious arrogance. Those who choose to embrace an exaggerated opinion of their talents or accomplishments have failed to temper themselves appropriately. Life teaches us that the dishwasher is just as critical to the success of a 5-star restaurant as the head waiter. Every man in a unit, every part of a well-oiled machine is equally important to the whole's success, and each person holds an equal share in the glory. When a person has mastered the ability to recognize their own limitations, while at the same time respecting and appreciating the gifts everyone else brings to the table, they are exhibiting the self-restraint and discipline needed to conquer their own demons and be of better service to others.

TEMPERANCE IN THE MARINES

The warrior's mentality is meant for those who want to become better and stronger; who aim to display self-restraint in thought, act and feeling. The warrior mentality is incompatible with a person whose lifestyle is focused only on improving their own place or status at the expense of others, or who adopts an arrogant attitude in place of humility.

Temperance is seen in the person who is mindful and in control of their actions, aware of how their actions affect themselves and others, and just as importantly, how their actions influence the mission at hand. Military members of all branches are rightly proud of the work they do and the training they've endured. That pride extends beyond the boundaries of one specific branch to another…though their way of acknowledging warriors from another team can sometimes resemble a game of verbal tennis gone bad, full of playful insults and colorful language.

GROWING UP IN *western Pennsylvania, Matt Bloom was 21 when he enlisted in the Marines. Ask him, and he'll says it was his military experience that brought out the good in him—more than he would have found on his own. He saw immediately that boot camp takes away the color of your skin, your socioeconomic status, and anything else that labelled you on the outside. Diverse groups were treated equally; dignity was ever-present, and justice was extended to all, across the board.*

Bloom is grateful for the lessons his military experience taught him; given the choice to do it all over again, he wouldn't hesitate. With speed and efficiency, he entered the ranks of the Field Military Police (MP), where his job was to provide immediate support for infantry (called grunts). The Field MPs worked alongside the grunts—same fire power, same maneuvers, same exercises, same operations—just with badges, though this was not your typical police work. Eventually their job was to receive, process, and transport EPWs, (enemy prisoners of war).

Bloom remembers putting temperance into play in his experience during the Second Battle of Fallujah,

Iraq (November 2004). Following orders requires self-discipline; if a commanding officer gives an order or tells you to do something, you do it. This is because the intense discipline developed, and strict lessons learned in boot camp get muddled when leadership fails. When you know that the direction you've been given—or lack thereof— are blatantly unsatisfactory or fail to account for the good of your fellow warriors, that's a significant problem—one that nobody wants to experience, especially not on the front lines under fire. If there's a weak link in leadership in times of military conflict, people can die.

Before the battle started, Bloom's unit was located 3 miles outside the city of Fallujah at the Forward Operating Base Camp Baharia. The Marines named Camp Baharia after they took it over from the U.S Army in 2004. As events progressed, at one point Bloom and some in his unit ended up bunking with 2nd Reconnaissance Marines. Recon Marines gather intelligence on the enemy and take out high value targets. They also work with civilian populations to gain intel on the enemy. This was a special high skills unit—2nd Marine Division, Marine Corps Special Forces—and Bloom and his unit were looking forward to meeting them and learning from them.

One day, a loud episode filled the air with irate voices and commotion—Bloom recalls it taking a few seconds to figure out what was going on—when one of the 2nd

Reconnaissance teams got trapped. The 2nd Recon were desperate for assistance and Matt's unit had equipment they needed and could use; what's more, they were ready and willing to come to their aid, fully understanding the significance of the 2nd Recon asking them for help. But Bloom was disgusted and flabbergasted when one of the staff sergeants in charge wouldn't give the order to assist—even after the 2nd Recon requested it directly. Bloom recalls that his personal temperance came into play, as he showed self-restraint by not acting out, creating additional turmoil—or mutiny, to use his term. He knew there was no righting this wrong, and he felt constrained at this point because of ineffective leadership; but he followed orders. To do otherwise would only add to the problem.

It wouldn't be the last time a lack of orders, refusal to engage and an unwillingness to lead would be displayed by the higher-ups on scene. But this time, when those same staff sergeants again shirked their duty to command and lead, it was during a situation that could end with loss of life. This time, Buzz was present as well as Bloom—at Checkpoint 84, another operating base outside Fallujah. The plan was to run what are called "feints": military operations intended to confuse and mislead the enemy through the use of tricks, ruses and psychological warfare. Ten days out from the set date for the invasion, they gathered the convoys and purposefully moved implements up and down the road, acting as though they'd started their invasion in hopes of exposing the enemy's position.

While out on maneuver one night, the convoys started taking fire, escalating into a dangerous and life-threatening situation in a hurry. When the request was made to the two platoon sergeants to engage and return fire, their inexplicable answer was, "No." Fully frustrated and fed up in the heat of the moment, someone pulled one of the platoon sergeants off his weapon on top of the Humvee and took his place as gunner, and immediately—with no hesitation—began returning enemy fire.

Later, Bloom and others knew they had to do something about this lack of leadership before someone got killed. It had now become an issue of safety and survival. As similar stories involving the same commanding officers and all-too-familiar endings accumulated, Bloom, along with the other squad leaders and vehicle commanders, went to Buzz and another 1st Sergeant who took the ineffective platoon sergeants off their missions. Bloom and other vehicle commanders—Reiher, Wolf, Cochran and Downs—were put in charge. Through this experience, they learned to successfully fine-tune their own leadership skills—and in so doing, discovered the warrior within.

Justice served.

TEMPERANCE: THE ENEMY

To defeat your enemy, you first have to know your enemy. When there is a lack of temperance, the following warning signs appear:

- **(X) Failing to understand the "big picture" situation**. Unable to appreciate or see all the variables that go into the decision-making process.

- **(X) Not knowing the right time to speak or stay silent**. Inappropriate engagement in sensitive situations.

- **(X) No awareness of personal and professional limits**; talking too much.

- **(X) Carelessness**; allowing self-destructive and unsafe behaviors in yourself.

- **(X) Poor bearing**. Being overly permissive with your loved ones. Being inappropriate or acting impulsively in professional settings.

- **(X) Being rash, quick to anger, impulsive or wild**; agitation. Failure to keep urges in check; inability to proceed cautiously.

- **(X) Drinking and eating in excess**; indulgence. Abuse of substances; includes over-the-counter remedies, sleep aids, prescription medications and illegal drugs.

- **(X) Consumer stupidity**; buying stuff because it makes you happy in the moment. Building up college, home, car, credit card debt without a plan to pay things off.

⊗ **Acting overly entitled**, whether towards material items or titles and respect.

⊗ **Exhibiting virtuous warrior behavior without purpose or cause**; "virtue signaling".

TEMPERANCE: 9-LINE REPORT

We've identified the enemy. What's our plan of action?

1. **Check in:** Determine where things stand. Where am I? How fast am I going? Am I able to be present, to appreciate the moment? Define your goal, recognize what you want. As you do so, recognize that your actions and decisions affect others around you.

2. **Identify:** Determine what will serve as the basis of your actions. Acting out of impatience, impulsiveness, arrogance and selfishness will only prevent temperance from being your focus.

3. **Prioritize:** There is a time and a place for snap decisions—no one's denying that. But if you find the majority of your decisions need to be made in a split-second, you're not practicing proper temperance in your dealings. Focus on the actions and consequences—good and bad, long term and short—of the decision you're about to make. If they aren't for the greater good, then trust your gut: it's probably not a good decision.

4. **Make a plan:** Planning temperance is not necessarily about making a decision. It's more a question of, "How can I be the best possible version of me?" One of the best planning strategies you can utilize is to play out any decision before you make it. What will happen immediately? How will others react? Will the desired outcome be achieved? And, most important: Will I be proud of my decision?

5 **Set goals:** When utilizing temperance, you won't necessarily have an end goal. Acting temperately is more foundational than that; your "goal" might therefore be to avoid arrogance. Or, your goal could include being a good person overall, aspiring to set a good example for those around you. Temperance not only means keeping your best interests in mind, but also protects your "team": your family, your friends, your co-workers, etc. Setting goals through temperance should therefore be thought of as an internal, personal goal—a declaration of the standard to which you will hold yourself. In doing so, you determine the level of effort you'll be putting forward in pursuing all other goals.

6 **Commit:** Temperance is a lifestyle. It's not something you can purchase or daydream into reality. To reach this point and acknowledge the change required demands effort and consistency.

7 **Execute:** We aren't suggesting anyone become Mother Theresa or the Dalai Lama. But by exercising good judgement, being a good person, and keeping others' best interests at the forefront, you are better served as well.

8 **Evaluate:** An evaluation of the short and long-term effects of temperance at play is always going to be a rolling account—there are no hard-and-fast successes (or failures) when aspiring to practice temperate behavior. You're looking to keep things in balance, which will form the framework of how you assess your progress.

⑨ Fire for effect: It's not always easy to say for certain what will occur once you've implemented temperance into your daily life. But you will start to notice changes in yourself. You'll have a more positive outlook on life; friends and family will compliment you at work and play. When you make a decision to take control of your life, the tough times become somehow easier. You're on the right path. Keep going and stay invested.

TEMPERANCE: SIT-REP

- **Study moderation in your actions and behaviors, as well as your personal thoughts and comments**. If you find yourself in an argument with someone, try counting to ten before speaking. Avoid the use of "I" statements.

- **Exhibit a dignified bearing in tense situations**. Be mindful, considerate of others and an active listener. Maintain eye contact. Be sincere and respectful. Practice personal control and management of excess.

- **Be humble and set a good example**; be grateful. Consistently say "Please" and "Thank you." Avoid false humility. When receiving a compliment on an obvious accomplishment, don't talk yourself down or belittle the task. That's just as bad as being unable to say, "Thank you." Avoid attention seeking.

- **Always bear in mind the Marine Corps motto**: Semper Fidelis, meaning "Always faithful." Be faithful to those to whom you have made a commitment, personal, financial or otherwise. Learn to forgive; let go of past events and stop harboring guilt or hatred.

- **Temper your desires and learn to curb your impulses.** If you are married or in a committed relationship, don't indulge in debilitating or self-destructive sexual activity. Practice the art of delayed gratification, saving money for a large purchase instead of putting it on a credit card and hoping the backyard money tree blossoms in the spring.

⚫ **Be cognizant of your nutrition and meal intake**. Avoid snacking between meals, processed foods and sugary beverages. Limit or reduce alcohol consumption. Avoid impulses and urges when drinking or under the influence of substances.

⚫ **Avoid over-consumption**; stop purchasing things that you don't need. Keep your attire to a minimal functioning collection, avoiding any excess of items you won't wear.

⚫ **Moderate time with your mobile devices, videos games, and television.** Try to make the best use of your time by pursuing things that stimulate and enrich, rather than just "killing time."

⚫ **Integrate health initiatives into your lifestyle**. Start living a healthy lifestyle, embracing a holistic approach where possible. Commit to developing your emotional intelligence.

4

CHARITY

"In a room where people unanimously maintain a conspiracy of silence, one word of truth sounds like a pistol shot."
—CZESLAW MILOSZ, POET

THE CONCEPT OF charity originated in ancient times—a form of love, which together with faith and hope makes up the three theological virtues. When we think of charity in modern times, we immediately think of financial charity—dropping a few dollars in the bucket around the holidays before getting on with our lives. But charity is so much more—and so much more important—than that. Charity is the practice of giving goodness and positivity to others, particularly to those in need or less fortunate than ourselves, often without the expectation of receiving anything in return. And while charity is frequently received in the form of goods and services, charity takes many forms depending on the recipient's needs. There are those who value the time we spend with them far more than any material goods.

CHARITY AS ACTION

Charity as action provides a unique opportunity for all of us, young and old, to better the life of another person. There are many available options for giving and receiving in today's society; charity has evolved in contemporary times to exist as a thing, an institution, as well as an action or a feeling of generosity toward those in need. Foundations set up by those who have lost loved ones are just one example of charitable giving, and are without a doubt a large undertaking even for those with the financial backing.

CHARITY IN THE MARINES

In 1947, just a few years after the end of World War II, Los Angeles residents Major Bill Hendricks and his wife Diane made a decision—a commitment to a cause during the Christmas season that endures to this day, thanks to the Marine Corps Reserve.

That commitment was the Toys for Tots program, which got its start the day Diane Hendricks gave her husband his marching orders: to deliver some dolls she had made to a local agency focused on children in need. (Many a great Marine has an even better spouse beside them, and Diane Hendricks was no exception—the motivating yin to Marine Corps reservist Bill's yang.)

To Bill's dismay, he couldn't find any agency or organization in the Los Angeles area that accepted donations of this nature. He was forced to return to base and announce to his wife that he had failed in his mission. But when he reported his findings to Diane, she fired back with, "Start one!"

And so he did just that. Major Hendricks' Marines in Los Angeles were responsible for collecting over 5,000 toys that inaugural Christmas, and Toys for Tots went national the next year. Now, annually during the holiday season bins and boxes fill up with donated unwrapped toys that are then distributed to families who cannot afford to buy Christmas presents for their own kids. These bins can be found in retail environments, common areas of shopping malls, and are prominently displayed at U.S. Post Offices and other local businesses. And collecting and distributing these toys are members of the Marine Corps—Benas, Bloom and Buzz included.

When Benas, Bloom and Buzz were assigned the job of collecting bins full of donated toys and stacking them in a local Pittsburgh warehouse for distribution, it was just another responsibility to carry out. A task to check off the list—nothing to put much thought into.

They had only limited intel on the donation program's back story and knew little of its lasting significance. But with hindsight comes wisdom, and now that day they worked together is a moment in time that all three warriors, now settled down with jobs and families and lives of their own thousands of miles apart from each other, will forever cherish.

When Benas, Bloom and Buzz recall the work done that year, it brings them continued hope and good memories during the Christmas season. The men reflect back on the Marines' wives, girlfriends, husbands and boyfriends who worked with them that day, just as Diane had alongside her husband. The sight of the toy-filled bins and boxes on display every year sticks with them like super glue and acts as a reminder to be just and treat people with fairness and dignity.

SIMPLE ACTS OF CHARITY

What we tend to consider smaller acts of charity—extending kindness in the form of a friendly smile to a random stranger, for example—provide just as significant an opportunity to improve the world around us every day. Cleaning out your closets and making a run to your local Goodwill or homeless shelter; giving away shoes you no longer use or have outgrown to a neighbor's kids; depositing goods in the bin labeled for give-away outside the grocery store; these are common, everyday examples of charity. Giving money to churches or community food banks, animal shelters, or large or small non-profit organizations is another way to give of yourself to those in need. In the digital era, websites like GoFundMe provide an online service to help those who need help paying their rent or medical bills.

CHARITY AND TEMPERANCE

Charity and temperance are virtues which go hand-in-hand. Giving of ourselves until we have nothing left isn't a sound tactical decision; so, for all that we are taught from childhood to always give from the heart, the head must also be consulted before making any decision to act charitably.

Before giving financially, we must be certain we are in a position to do so. And sometimes we aren't; if it's a decision between giving to an animal shelter and paying the rent, your responsibility is to take care of yourself, lest you become as in-need as those you're trying to help. There will always be more opportunities to practice the virtue of charity. If you can't spare the money, see if you can spare some old hand-me-downs. If you can't spare anything material, give of your time. If you can't even do that, then spread the word, raising awareness for those in need.

Goodness exists in every corner of the world. The Marine philosophy includes taking care of the one on your left and on your right, providing a clear path towards a better life for all. Charity is a warrior virtue as important as any other, and by understanding and implementing charity in our daily living, we strengthen ourselves and our society as a whole.

CHARITY: THE ENEMY

To defeat your enemy, you first have to know your enemy. When there is a lack of charity, the following warning signs appear:

- **X** **Inequity**; evil and unfair acts.

- **X** **Disservice**; doing wrong by others.

- **X** **Dishonesty**; lying to both yourself and others, ignoring personal imperfections that you should be working to improve.

- **X** **Favoritism**; judging others' behavior, their personal situations.

- **X** **A lack of honor**; acting inappropriately towards others; refusing to cooperate with others; then scolding others for their actions.

- **X** **Inaction**. Ruthlessness; laziness or cruelty presented as apathy.

- **X** **Jealousy**; selfishness, taking from others.

- **X** **Being vindictive**; showing retaliatory or discriminatory behavior; spewing vitriol through email, text or via social media.

- **X** **Demonstrating a lack of compassion**; being unsupportive in the face of real need.

CHARITY: 9-LINE REPORT

We've identified the enemy. What's our plan of action?

1 **Check in:** Determine exactly what decision needs to be made; for example, in Major Hendricks' case, where can the dolls and toys be taken?

2 **Identify:** What makes the decision unique, requiring additional thought or planning? In this instance, there is no distributing organization, meaning there was nowhere to take the toys.

3 **Prioritize:** Keep your end goals clear in your mind as you determine how best to move forward. Whatever plan you make should prioritize the success of whichever element is most mission-critical.

4 **Make a plan:** Assess your available resources, as well as any unique ways in which those resources can be utilized, and create a blueprint for success that takes full advantage of your options.

5 **Set goals:** When planning for success, keep the long-term in mind. What can be gained in the short-term? What can be done to ensure the most benefit for the most people?

6 **Commit:** Once your decision is made, move forward. Adapt to the situation as it develops; don't waste time second-guessing yourself into complete paralysis.

7 **Execute:** Put the plan into action. This is where your resources are utilized and your manpower committed. Be ready for anything, but trust in the work you've put in leading up to this point.

8 **Evaluate:** Did it work? Was the success in a smaller scale than expected? Could you have pushed yourself harder, made it farther? It doesn't matter; success paves the way for future success.

9 **Fire for effect:** Having taken stock of everything, how can you improve next time? How can you make your charity event bigger, your toy drive more successful, your outreach more visible?

CHARITY: SIT-REP

(√) **Act in service to others**. Learn how to give, especially to those who cannot return the favor.

(√) **Treat people the way you would like to be treated—with respect and dignity**. Treat people with honesty and act with personal integrity in your personal dealings. Never allow anyone in your presence to be mistreated. When something isn't right, speak up about it.

(√) **Keep family, friends, colleagues and your community as your priority, over and above yourself**. Don't seek happiness just for yourself; help others be happy and you will receive happiness in ways you could never expect.

(√) **Get involved with causes you are passionate about**. Start small and build upon initial successes. Avoid burnout to provide maximum benefit to as many people as possible.

(√) **Get rid of the stuff cluttering your home that could be of better use to someone else**. This includes clothing, kitchen items, books, tools and appliances. Provide in-kind donations, where your company donates products and services in exchange for monetary donations and sponsorships.

(√) **Donate your time, energy, resources and knowledge**. The things you have in abundance to share are likely things that someone else desperately needs. Organize community events to leverage more volunteers and resources. Donate blood. Volunteer at shelters. Become a pen pal with warriors fighting abroad, sending holiday greeting cards to those injured or those battling illness at home. Prep meals and deliver them to those in need through services like Meals on Wheels. Become a Big Brother or Sister to those in need of an adult figure or mentor. The possibilities are as endless as the need.

5

FORTITUDE

"The greater the difficulty, the more glory in surmounting it. Skillful pilots gain their reputation from storms and tempests."

—EPICTETUS, GREEK STOIC PHILOSOPHER

FORTITUDE IS MENTAL and emotional strength in the face of adversity. It's a woman doing box jumps on a prosthetic leg; it's the man in the prime of his life who just got the news that his son, a young father himself, was suddenly killed in a random car accident, and that he's on the hook to pick up his dead son's 5-year-old at daycare and tell him his dad is gone; it's the warrior who busts their ass to do their job even while taking fire.

Fortitude is also the discipline to control one's self during times of extreme uncertainty and intimidation; the oftentimes extraordinary ability to tuck your fear away and do the right thing, with no thought of one's own safety or even if the outcome is guaranteed. The type of acts that elicit "oohs" and "ahhs" when someone witnesses such a display of personal strength. Fortitude is the ability to "buck up," to summon one's courage; but it also means being afraid and going into the lion's den anyway.

When one has the self-discipline and the ability to confront fear and continue to act as they should, they are operating with bravery, courage and fortitude.

CULTIVATING FORTITUDE

It might sound a bit odd, to talk about building up fortitude like it were a muscle to work out or a skill to hone. It seems easier—or at least more convenient—to think of fortitude as something you're born with, an inherent inner strength that you either have or you don't. Increasing one's fortitude sounds like "learning to be brave" or "studying determination"; it all sounds a bit too vague.

The reason for this is that personal change often occurs below the surface, and at a rate too slow for most people to notice—at least, until something unexpected happens and we surprise ourselves with how we respond, both positively and negatively. If you spend each day lazing around, making nothing of yourself and letting every opportunity pass you by, only to be suddenly thrust into a position where you have to make a lot of hard decisions in a short amount of time, odds are you'll be completely overwhelmed, to the point where you shut down and can't function.

But if you spend each day engaging with those around you, meeting your deadlines at work or completing your assignments at school, advancing your knowledge or improving your skills bit by bit, you will be shocked at how well you deal with unexpected challenges. And even then, you might not notice how you've landed on your feet, or how you already have some ideas of what to do or who to turn to, because it's all just a natural extension of the life you've lived up to that point.

Developing fortitude isn't easy, but neither is it complex. In the same way that people will tell you to dress for the job you want, the simple acts of practicing good habits, always facing things head on and striving to push yourself just that one extra step further each day will, in the long run, reap tremendous benefits. Just because there are no outward appearances that you are growing stronger, trust that all the hard work you've put into yourself will come through for you in a big way when you need it most.

BORN IN 1969, Buzz's upbringing, personality and conscience always demanded full and active engagement in what mattered. He was never one to sit still and observe; in fact, his mother talks about how the baby inside her "buzzed"…and the moniker stuck. His father is a Vietnam combat vet and spent 35 years with the Philadelphia fire department; his grandfather was Army and served in the infantry in Europe.

In addition, Buzz is a product of Field Medical Training School, Camp Johnson, Marine Corps Base Camp Lejeune—a Navy man who retired after 22 years of service. (In the Marine Corps, there are no medics; the Navy provides all medical personnel to a Marine Corps unit.)

Buzz's personality is one that busts the proverbial door down, and it suits him well. Dangerous jobs, unsafe jobs—it didn't matter, if what's in front of him needs addressing, he seizes it without hesitation. He's the type who picks out the new guys and figures them out, getting to know their temperament ahead of time. He wants to know that if he says, "Get your head down," the other guy will get his head down.

That was the environment he lived and worked in. In his world, you're engaged and dialed in, no questions asked. You do the right thing, the end.

So it was no surprise when Buzz volunteered for a convoy that would be departing Al Asad, becoming part of the long, slow and snaking line of tactical vehicles, oil tankers, and five-ton trucks carrying troops on its way to the hot spot of Ramadi. Ramadi was a strategic hub for access to the Euphrates River, and major inroads to Syria and Jordan—a very desirable land grab for members of the insurgency and coalition.

Suddenly, before the last vehicle's rubber could reach safe ground, their crawl came to an abrupt halt when an IED detonated and hit one of the five-ton transports with troops in the back. It was a solid hit; rocket-propelled grenades were now being shot in their direction, and they were taking small arms fire. The enemy had effectively disabled the Humvee and they couldn't get it out of the kill zone.

Time stops. Thirty seconds seems like 30 hours. The questions come fast and furious, pinballing around your brain: "Who's shooting?" "Is everything still attached?"

"Is my arm or leg wet?" "Who got hit? Was it a buddy or another Marine?"

Buzz quickly realized the questions flying through his head didn't matter. He trusted his people and he was going to do everything in his power to get them out alive. Buzz's laser focus kicked in within a millisecond. Once in that mode of operation, you no longer see the distractions on the periphery; you simply act. He locates an injured Marine and applies a tourniquet. He can smell the blood, he knows it's a traumatic amputation. But he just hooks up an IV and moves on. The trick in situations like this is to be fast and efficient, tamp down the emotions (which are running high), and trust your people to work effectively in an environment demanding hyper vigilance.

Buzz's take on this episode is pragmatic, and one that demands taking ownership. You work. You dump your gear and you go to work. He remembers how, after months and months of learning and practicing, he still wondered how it would go down in real time. The rules of engagement in Iraq weren't initially clear: you never knew who you could trust, with folks getting shot even under white flag conditions. A Unit First Sergeant even told him and the rest of the unit, "You shoot first. Beg for forgiveness later," saying this was better than second guessing yourself and ending up in a bag. Buzz decided, moving forward, that's how he would operate. If the *mission dictated, he'd do things differently, but for the good of the mission, he'd do what was expected of him.*

"You're capable of more than you give yourself credit for." How many times have we heard that line, or something close to it? It's safe to say that the majority of people aren't living up to their full potential on a day to day basis.

But it's also safe to say that most people don't face situations in their daily life that push them as far as they'll go, and then some. The limits of what a human being can do given the right set of circumstances—of which a combat situation is one example—are amazing, and should give each of us a greater sense of hope and confidence in ourselves.

Cultivating fortitude means pushing our personal envelope. It means raising the ceiling on our personal limits, so that when the time comes—and it comes for everyone who doesn't live in a bubble or under a rock—we're ready for the worst life can throw at us. Like flossing your teeth or taking your vitamins, it's a preventative measure—preparation for a day to come when all the strength we've been building will be needed. Remember that complacency kills. Running from valor creates an enemy that will haunt you forever, while defeating that enemy will serve as an unimaginable source of personal pride and success.

We are each of us called to be tested, at some point. Don't try to cram the night before—spend each day preparing, and be ready.

FORTITUDE: THE ENEMY

To defeat your enemy, you first have to know your enemy. When there is a lack of fortitude, the following warning signs appear:

- **Retreating from all areas of life**; avoidance behavior; seeking comfort in the face of pain.

- **Fear**; be it of the unknown, of the future, of death, of others' opinions or judgements, of screwing things up, of injury, or even of your own shadow.

- **Self-absorption**; an inability to think of anyone but yourself. Exhibiting an obsession with one's self, with materialistic acknowledgment. Needing pats on the back for doing nothing.

- **Self-doubt**; an inability to make a decision; hesitation or paralyzing fear.

- **Micromanaging**; at home, with offspring or at work; blaming others for your actions.

- **Lack of faith**; having a pessimistic outlook, lack of trust, not trusting others.

- **Lack of a spine**; failure to stand up for yourself and/ or others.

- **Feeling stuck in a rut;** doing the same thing over and over and expecting different outcomes; allowing a need for personal comfort to disrupt and displace your life.

- **A lack of emotional restraint**; allowing your emotions to control the situation; exhibiting fear and allowing it to control your decision making and execution.

(X) **Being indifferent or removed from the mission at hand**; lacking perseverance to go on, to set and accomplish goals; not trusting your gut in decision making.

(X) **Lack of drive**; denying yourself employment or promotional opportunities; working beneath your capabilities, education and skillset.

FORTITUDE: 9-LINE REPORT

We've identified the enemy. What's our plan of action?

1 **Check in:** Acknowledge your fear for what it is. Understand its origins, know that it *can* get in the way, but it doesn't *need* to. Prepare to take action despite your fear. Lock down any emotional responses to a situation that needs to be addressed with logic. Above all, do not allow anger to disrupt your thinking at the critical moment.

2 **Identify:** What are the characteristics of the situation? What are the appropriate behaviors and actions called for? What are the variables? What is your goal? Start visualizing the *ideal* outcome.

3 **Prioritize:** Visualize each element of the situation and rank them from most important to least important. This will allow you to act accordingly as the situation develops.

4 **Make a plan:** What needs to happen in order to achieve the desired result? Forget about yourself entirely, trusting that you will have the fortitude to accomplish what the situation asks of you.

5 **Set goals:** With a plan in place, once again visualize the *ideal* outcome. Does it align with your values?

6 **Commit:** Cement your decision. Now is the time to visualize the final, or *likely* outcome. Stand tall and behave as though you have already achieved the desired final outcome.

7 **Execute:** Gather and maintain the courage needed in order to achieve results and the desired outcome.

8 **Evaluate:** What worked well? What did not go as planned? Avoid placing blame, either on yourself or others. Take ownership of failures, take pride in successes. Focus on improving for the next go-around.

9 **Fire for effect:** Live. Learn. Repeat. Commit to the process of becoming a better version of yourself. Accept that this process is never ending and constantly evolving. You *will* become stronger, so long as you work towards it.

FORTITUDE: SIT-REP

√ **Speak up against what is not right.** Be brave and calculating even in challenging situations. Act in a just manner; this gives you steady ground to stand tall upon. Never waver in your stance against others; remain true to your personal convictions.

√ **Obliterate obstacles with patience, persistence and perseverance**. Continue to persevere in the face of adversity, pain, fear and danger. Tamp down excessive emotions during times of duress.

√ **Resist temptation and avoid over-extending yourself.** Learn to say "No" often and "Yes" only when it is appropriate. Exercise self-control during times of uncertainty and extreme intimidation.

√ **Seize opportunities without hesitation**. Be fast and efficient in times of need. Know to abandon even your own safety when the situation warrants it.

√ **Embrace the mission, taking the time to understand all variables**. Enthusiasm is all well and good, but it fades with time; commit to truly appreciating what you're doing and stay engaged.

√ **Face your enemies straight on**. Be they bullies, creditors, or personal vices like addiction. Answer the phone call, the email, the text message. Putting things off will only cost you more in the long run.

√ **Trust your team**, whether that is family, friends or co-workers, to carry out their particular tasks.

Stand up for yourself. Apply this principle to every aspect of your life. Commit to always doing what's expected of you, and place faith in your own abilities, training and planning.

6

DECISIVENESS

"The mind of Caesar. It is the reverse of most men's. It rejoices in committing itself. To us arrive each day a score of challenges: we must say yes or no to decisions that will set off chains of consequences. Some of us deliberate; some of us refuse the decision, which is itself a decision; some of us leap giddily into the decision, setting our jaws and closing our eyes, which is the sort of decision of despair. Caesar embraces decision. It is as though he felt his mind to be operating only when it is interlocking itself with significant consequences. Caesar shrinks from no responsibility. He heaps more and more upon his shoulders."

—Thornton Wilder, The Ides of March

VERY FEW INDIVIDUALS can walk into a job or onto an athletic field with no experience and expect to succeed. We train for a job, we go to school to gain skills, we practice free throws and hitting balls to get better. To be able to perform at a certain level of expertise, we understand that a certain level of prior experience is necessary. We also understand that to achieve that level of experience, we have to commit to seeking it out and sticking with it, even when the going gets rough. It's a fact that most anyone can pick up a basketball and shoot a basket. It doesn't mean that most anyone can go pro.

PRACTICE MAKES PERFECT

So, how can we improve to the point where we are good enough to succeed? The answer is as simple as it is unpleasant (at least to some): continuous repetition and exposure to the task. We practice, we do drills, we work to get better, smarter, faster and stronger.

The military as a whole does all this and more on a daily basis so that they can perform to the best of their ability in the heat of the moment. In that case, success is the difference between staying alive and completing the mission, or failing to do either. With optimum training comes optimum performance, and thus lives are saved and crucial battles are won. But optimum training is not something that comes easy; it's a result of people taking decisive action. Simply put, success is a result of practice and confidence.

PERFORMING UNDER FIRE

Many individuals can perform at a high level in their chosen field…at least, under ideal circumstances in a controlled environment. But to perform at a high level while under fire, in a high stress and unstable environment… that's another matter entirely.

But if you're going to put the time into developing your skills and building your experience base, you'd want those skills to serve you well even when your boss comes to you at 4:45 pm on a Friday needing a sales pitch completed for a high value customer ASAP. You'll want to be able to act calmly and decisively when you're a first responder at the site of your first multi-vehicle crash with many traumatic injuries.

Will you be ready? Are you able to jump into action, volunteering to make the sales pitch because you are confident in the skills you've honed? Or are you hiding in the corner, mentally paralyzed at the scene of a pile-up because you don't know where to begin or who to triage first? Indecisiveness takes over—not because you aren't knowledgeable, but because you lack training, or are unprepared for the sorts of high stress situations that require decisive action.

Many times, you will hear those in the military say things like, "We fight how we train." This is obviously best practice for combat situations, but the same principle can be applied to any walk of life. Life is full of pitfalls, most of them unexpected. And the only two things we can control are how well we prepare, and how confidently we meet the challenge when it comes. We don't care much for clichés in this book, but one that *is* appropriate here is: Prepare for the worst and hope for the best. If you're prepared and able to make hard but sound decisions in the face of adversity, you'll be more effective than those around you, keeping you ahead of the game.

Being able to take action in the critical moment is the difference between getting that promotion or pay raise. And we appreciate how hard in can be when the pressure's on, and you're standing in the crosshairs. But the point it that while no one is perfect at making decisions, decisions still need to be made. Some on the spot, some with greater care and thought; some trivial, some life-changing. But the most important common trait to any decision is action. If there is no action taken, then you are to blame for the outcome. No one else, you!

DECISIVENESS IN THE MARINES

Marines must make decisions quickly, processing information based on past histories of training doctrine, feedback from their fellow warriors and analysis of information from scouting and intelligence reports. Marines are decisive both in garrison and in the theatre of war, a quality that follows them to success in their civilian life.

In 1997, Benas recalls reading a magazine with a United States Marine, fully dressed in his service dress blues uniform, with officer's sword on full display. The premise of the article was that roughly 175 of the Fortune 500 companies that made the list that year were successfully run by former Marines. One would therefore argue that decisiveness would be predominant in that class of leaders.

Being decisive also requires that you be ethical in your decision making. This is more difficult in situations of ambiguity and chaos, such as seen in theatres of war. At times like these, the Marines are able to rely on the Corps' institutional values, as well as the personal values they've obtained along the way. It's important, both in life and business, that you don't compromise your values, cutting corners in times of great stress.

PRIOR TO DEPLOYING to Iraq in 2004, the authors' unit was doing some live fire shooting exercises at an Army base in Alabama. Standard Operating Procedure required a head count of Marines and Sailors, as well as checks on the methods, equipment, supplies, and vehicles prior to turning in for the day.

At 1730 hours (5:30 pm), 30 minutes past the anticipated end of training for that day, leaders Bloom, Ace Cochran and O'Neil had a dilemma. The platoon was missing a 40mm MK 19 round belonging to the type of automatic belt fed grenade launcher being fired that day on the range. Their moral dilemma was this: they could ignore the fact that one round had turned up missing, send everyone back to the barracks for warm chow, a hot shower, and some rest…or they could pull everyone to do a police call and search every square inch of the range, including the gear and vehicles that were used during training.

Bloom, Ace and O'Neil decided to make the ethical decision, and take the chance of compromising the morale of their platoon. There wasn't much light to work with, so they began searching every square inch with flashlights, combing the range and the Humvees where the MK 19 Grenade launchers were mounted.

It was now 2230 hours (10:30 pm) and still nothing. Meanwhile, the Marines were understandably disappointed that they were still up and continuing to work through their meals, hygiene and downtime. That long day went on for a few more hours until they found success.

By then, the Marines had realized the right decision had been made by their leaders, even at the compromise of their temporary comfort. They knew they could now count on these three to make the right decisions moving forward. Bloom, Ace and O'Neil had won—earned— their trust.

Being assertive, dispelling all hesitation, and applying speed and efficiency to decision making are must-haves for all great leaders. The Marines' mantra sums this up as, "*Smooth is fast.*" To put it another way, a disciplined laser focus makes for efficient and expedient decision makers who rise to the top. The ability to make sound and effective decisions separates us from the rest of the pack.

Most people will do whatever it takes to avoid making a decision. The majority of the population, military and civilian both, would much rather let others make decisions for them. Not to mention, our society as a whole is overwhelmed with options, each with their own variables to consider and scenarios to play out. Grocery store shelves paralyze us with fear and exhaustion, trying to pick out one choice from a dozen options. Large metro area car dealerships have every make, model and color of truck on the lot. Frustration mounts as we fail to come to a decision, eating away at our self-confidence and our drive.

We end up staying home, unwilling to make a call on anything. Instead, we harbor our insecurities and lack of self-confidence, worrying ourselves to distraction over what others think, when those others are just as consumed with their own fears and insecurities. We procrastinate, obsess over past decisions gone badly, analyzing and over-analyzing.

Worse, we make the mistake of handicapping ourselves with excuses. We hesitate, with disastrous results; we hinder ourselves when making decisions, then obsess about the negative outcome. Of course, making a decision doesn't mean we have a say in the outcome; we should always have a goal in mind, but we are only capable of doing the best we can at any given time. Too often we base our feeling of success or failure on the outcome. Credit is due to those who confidently make a right decision without concern for the outcome. If we do the right thing, our consciences are clear, and the image of ourselves we project remains authentic and inspiring.

DECISIVENESS: THE ENEMY

To defeat your enemy, you first have to know your enemy. When there is a lack of decisiveness, the following warning signs appear:

- **X** **Procrastination**; stalling, making excuses, hesitation, habitual delay and fear of commitment.

- **X** **Insecurity;** the inability to make decisions; hesitation; questioning everything and having uncertainty; worrying about others' opinions; an inability to give or receive criticism.

- **X** **Inappropriate passivity**, apathy; not being present in the moment; being stalled out, disjointed; lack of focus.

- **X** **Replacing important tasks with easy distractions**; accepting instant gratification and negativity that will result in events detrimental to your intended goals.

- **X** **Being ineffective**, not reliable enough to make decisions; avoiding the time it takes to learn a task or lifesaving principle that will propel you through life.

- **X** **Being overly certain, even when you don't know all the variables**; having a "shoot first" mentality; talking more than using your listening skills.

- **X** **Being submissive to others** and their misguided direction(s); appearing questionable in your authority; not projecting confidence.

DECISIVENESS: 9-LINE REPORT

We've identified the enemy. What's our plan of action?

1 **Check in:** What decision needs to be made? What is the nature of the situation calling for action, and what is the time table for response?

2 **Identify the issue:** What kind of decision is this? Life and death? A normal part of everyday life? Career oriented? Personal? Assess the magnitude of the decision and bear it in mind going forward.

3 **Prioritize:** Life does not methodically hand us one issue requiring our attention at a time, nor does it wait patiently for us to clear our inbox before giving us more. Life and death decisions are critically important, and even simpler decisions still need time to process and decipher. Avoid procrastinating and assess honestly, prioritizing what needs to be addressed first.

4 **Make a plan:** Create a list of pros and cons as a good starting point. This is also a good time to be selfish and consider what is best for you. Taking outside opinions or advice is also welcome and encouraged in this stage.

5 **Set goals:** What do I realistically hope to achieve from the outcome of this decision? A positive outcome is not guaranteed, as it is out of your control. Being prudent and wise in decision making will always be more advantageous than betting on a positive outcome, as it leaves you in a more tenable position afterwards.

6 **Commit:** Follow through on your plan. Indecisiveness just means the issue will linger. Visualize clearing the puddle or stream by jumping over it.

7 **Execute the plan:** Stick to your decision and take any appropriate action needed while making your decision. At this point, you may have to address any adverse or positive consequence of the decision.

8 **Evaluate:** Acknowledge what worked and what didn't work. Did I miss anything in my pros or cons? Did something come in from left field and upend my plan? Were there unintended consequences? Make adjustments as needed with your goal in mind.

9 **Fire for effect:** Making a solid decision in one instance will lead to additional good decisions in the future. Life experience makes us better. You're still moving forward on the path to greatness. Don't stop here; continue on!

DECISIVENESS: SIT-REP

- ✓ **Make that uncomfortable decision you've been putting off**. Do it now—decide! Build self-confidence by throwing yourself into new situations consistently in order to learn and grow.

- ✓ **Take charge, be assertive**. Don't sit around waiting for others to decide. Keep an eye on any outside factors and variables beyond your control that might have an impact on your decisiveness.

- ✓ **Make your decisions calculated and calm, but swift and final**. The worst decision you can make is no decision at all. Remove any and all hesitation. Remember, slow is smooth, but *smooth is fast*.

- ✓ **Be cognizant of how your actions impact you or others in your care**. This will save you time by preventing second-guessing down the road.

- ✓ **Learn to cut through the clutter quickly.** Try to slice through all the options presented to you when you go into any given situation.

- ✓ **Start by tackling little goals**, those that require an immediate decision; do not be paralyzed by the options. Then, turn those little goals into bigger and better goals that help with building your self-confidence and self-worth.

- ✓ **Be a leader**. When you're out with a group of people and are faced with what to eat, be the one to take charge so you don't continue to waste time. Everyone is looking for a way out in the hopes that someone will lead—*be* that decision maker.

√ **Keep your focus on the desired outcome of a decision and why you are trying to achieve it**. When you are decisive, events will happen for you. Do not compromise your own values in the decision-making process.

√ **Eliminate biases, old judgments, personal interests or others' opinions**. Don't allow outside influences to hold you back. Take in all the facts, data and intel about your situation and move *forward*.

7

HOPE

"You make your future. Don't hope and wait for something to drop into your lap. Make it happen."
— MASTER GUNNERY SERGEANT GUADALUPE DENOGEAN

"Many words are poverty."
— SPARTAN PROVERB

KNOWN AS ONE of the three theological virtues, hope is the optimistic anticipation of a situation's outcome. It is the expectation of fulfillment or success; it's what we do when we envision or anticipate something good, positive or productive happening for ourselves or for another person. Hope is looking forward to a brighter future. As such, hope is inherently a desire for good. It is the means by which we respond to the basic questions of the human struggle. Cultivating the virtue of hope means strengthening your very real capability of perseverance.

There's a real sense of fulfillment when we cultivate hope, for all those involved. We hope a patient is cancer-free; we hope our team wins the pennant; we hope our plan for the mission is executed; we hope the war ends. Hope is one way we can express our concerns and love for one another. Even in our darkest hours, hope keeps us going and moving to complete our goals, to execute the tasks at hand, to go from a bad situation to a better one, from a better situation to an optimum result.

To live with hope is to live with the anticipation that our ship is always just around the corner, just about to come in. We go about our business every day, seeing to our tasks and responsibilities, our jobs, school, places to go, things to do, bills to pay, appointments to keep, errands to run, without giving much thought to what lies ahead. Until we get thrown a curveball, that is; it could be news of a tragic accident involving a friend or relative, a home eviction, an unexpected medical diagnosis, or the loss of a job that is holding a household together.

The list of life's curveballs is long and unpredictable, and they don't discriminate. No one gets out of this life unscathed. Everyone's got their forest to fight through. So, how do we extricate ourselves from our dark moments and dire circumstances?

BENAS COMPLETED EVERYTHING *the Marine Corps asked of him. His enlistment ended in November 2002, prior to which he had proudly served with 1st Marine Division, 1st Tank Battalion, as a Marine Corps Martial Arts Instructor and Military Police Officer with 29 Palm's Provost Marshal's Office. He returned to civilian life and in January 2003 was settling into his undergraduate studies at Southern Connecticut State University.*

But that March, he began to receive messages from his fellow Marines who were still serving. 1st Tank Battalion was going to be the first Marine unit to deploy and lead the assault north into Baghdad, Iraq. America was at war, and Benas' friends were still fighting it. Marines were doing what they were designed to do; not training, but combat.

The reality of the situation, knowing that his fellow Marines were putting their lives on the line while Benas was physically able to join them gnawed on his conscience even as he attended college in the comfort and safety of the United States. As Benas reflected on his life in Connecticut, he thought of his friends doing what they'd committed themselves to achieving when they volunteered, sweat, and bled to become United States Marines. They were hoping that, in the crucible of combat when they were confronted with the austere brutality of war, they would possess the fortitude and discipline to uphold the highest standard of honor.

The Marines' goals weren't related to fame or wealth; they sought something miles higher, broader, and deeper than anything even remotely material. They sought to give the gift of security and freedom to others, regardless of whether it took a year of their life, their minds, their arms, their legs, or their very lives. They hoped they would earn the honor of applying everything they'd learned and trained to become in the arena of modern warfare.

CULTIVATING HOPE

Hope is a difficult thing to deliberately cultivate. As anyone who has gone through a traumatic situation can tell you, it's a challenge to try to regain hope after losing it. Hope is an outlook on life, a state of mind—if you don't feel hopeful about the future, you can't just tell yourself you do and expect to change your own way of thinking overnight.

What's more, hope is understood to be based on something, whether it's an expectation (reasonable or otherwise) or a personal goal or desire. That's what differentiates hope from faith: hope has a specific focus. But when situations change and the things we hope for become less and less likely, we feel like we're forced to either abandon hope or settle for less.

The good news is that there *are* ways to build hope—healthy, supportive ways that improve you as a person, rather than harmful ways that do little besides string you along. The problem gambler, for example, may hope that the next batch of lottery tickets will make him a millionaire—but that's definitely not the kind of hope we're going for!

First, take a step back and self-assess. Because hope is something that is born from a specific desire or goal, it's all too easy to wind up with tunnel vision, to the point where our happiness lives and dies by the outcome of whatever we're hoping for. In most cases, life is nowhere near that narrow: things that you've neglected—good things—are all around you. Maybe it's your relationships, romantic or platonic; maybe it's your professional life, where you still have the respect of your peers; maybe it's your personal life, where you still have stimulating hobbies and friend groups. There are so many opportunities for self-actualization and happiness in life that if you find yourself feeling hopeless, you might want to turn your head slightly to the left or right to see everything you're missing.

After you've assessed everything, if you're still feeling hopeless try telling yourself that everything's going to be great, that there *is* plenty to hope for. If you can spend all day telling yourself that everything's gone to hell and feel miserable as a result, it stands to reason that the reverse is true, right? Things like positive visualization and affirmations may not move mountains, but they help make sure you start things off on the right foot.

And that's the key: after you've done everything you can to start off on the right foot, you still have to *take that step*. This is where the line between being hopeful and cultivating hope is drawn: in whether or not you're able to pull it all together and take action.

SHORTLY AFTER THE *Marines began their assault north toward Baghdad, Benas' mentor Master Gunnery Sergeant Guadalupe Denogean was performing routine checks on his tank recovery vehicle in Basrah, Iraq. He climbed on top of the vehicle and began to wipe down the 50-caliber machine gun after a light mist of humidity had settled on the weapon during the night. He greeted the pigeons that were caged near the machine gun (there to warn of chemical attack), but as Denogean worked to ensure the machine gun was operational and ready for contact, a person in a nearby village launched a rocket propelled grenade in his direction. It landed two feet from him and detonated directly on top of the tank recovery vehicle.*

Shrapnel filled Denogean's body. He lost his hearing and parts of his hands. The bones in his leg shattered. He suffered a traumatic brain injury and later a stroke. His fellow Marines, those in or near the vehicle, were also injured by the blast. One of them was Corporal Phillip Randall Rugg II who later lost one of his legs as a result of his injuries. But despite his fellow Marines writhing in their own agonies, they ensured Denogean made it out of Basrah alive.

As Denogean recovered from his injuries in various military medical facilities, high ranking military and political officials filled the hallways outside his hospital room. One day, an official asked Denogean if he had any requests. Denogean paused to consider this question from the high ranking official and remembered something he'd been hoping for more than 26 years of his service in the United States Marine Corps. Denogean responded that he would like to become a citizen of the United States of America, the country he'd served for nearly three decades before almost losing his life that night in Basrah.

As a child, Denogean had dreamed of being a United States Marine after family members read accounts in Mexican newspapers of the bravery of Marines during combat in Vietnam. He was a resident alien when he enlisted in the Marine Corps as a young man. He'd applied for citizenship countless times during his decades of service in the Marine Corps, only to be stymied by a bureaucratic quagmire. As Denogean changed duty stations every few years, he was continually being set back in the bureaucratic process and lost his application fee every time.

Eventually, he stopped trying…until the high-ranking government official stood over him, asking if he had any requests. Denogean later said about his request, "There were Congressmen and Senators running around all over the place, so I figured, 'What the hell, you know?'"

Denogean's request was approved, and less than a week later President George W. Bush walked into his hospital room. Not only did Denogean receive a Purple Heart, but he also received his citizenship. Something he'd hoped for 26 years became a reality in less than

72 hours. Denogean also received word that another of his requests had been granted: Corporal Phillip Randall Rugg II, who had helped Denogean survive his injuries while dealing with the agony of his own broken legs, was being promoted to Sergeant at Denogean's request.

Six months later, Denogean, Benas, and Kevin Almeida, a former Sergeant in the same unit, were visiting together in Denogean's garage. Although Benas and Almeida were no longer Marine subordinates to Denogean, he gave an order: the three thirty-racks of beer in the garage needed to be finished before Benas and Almeida left. They drank the beer and shared countless stories into the night, reminiscing about the good times they'd shared when they were all in the same unit. They listened attentively as Master Gunns shared his experiences from nearly 30 years of Marine Corps service that spanned the Persian Gulf War and the most recent war in Iraq. Denogean's new hearing aids helped him to hear as they talked.

As Denogean shared with Benas his Purple Heart, Benas was overwhelmed with emotion. In the presence of his mentor, a true legend who had spent four years training Benas how to not only be a phenomenal Marine, but to be a man of honor and commitment, Benas knew what his conscience demanded of him. He decided that although there was no law, regulation, or military order requiring him to re-enlist, he would volunteer to go back into the Marine Corps to join his unit serving in Iraq.

He would go into the jaws of war, where no one and nothing besides his conscience demanded him to go. Benas would rejoin his friends and make new ones, friends like Bloom and Buzz, as they faced the violence, trauma, and uncertainty of war together.

Benas had hoped to live a life of honor and commitment, free of regrets. If he was killed in combat, at least his conscience would be clear, light, and free, knowing he'd fulfilled his duty to himself, his fellow Marines, and his country. He could lay hold of the object of his hope and join the ranks of men and women who shared the same sacred, burning desire. He sought to earn the respect and acceptance of those who'd lived like Denogean, with a love and reverence so deep that it transcends talk and operates only in the realm of action.

The ancient Spartans had a proverb: "Many words are poverty." In other words, people are known to talk at great length, and their words can be long, flowing rivers of sound, but still have little to no real value. Never has this been more true than in our own Information Age, a time of posts, likes, and anonymous comments. The Spartans knew that great men and women prove who they are with their actions, demonstrating what kind of character they possess through their deeds. Their words may be few, but both their actions and inactions demonstrated power.

Even decades later, Denogean lives in tremendous daily pain from his wounds. Yet he still remembers the bond he shares with Benas and how priceless it is. After reflecting on his life and the Marines he served with, Denogean told an interviewer: "Tell Nick I'd do anything for him. He knows that."

The hope of a Marine becomes action, until what they hope for becomes reality. No one will ever be able to take that from them.

Hope can be elusive. For all of us, at some point in our lives, there will come a time when all hope seems lost, where there is no ray of light in the darkness. The key is to not despair—to never give up. Find a way to persevere. Surround yourself with people who inspire you to be better, with people who build bridges instead of burning them. Take in movies, books and other media that inspire you with positivity and the warm fuzzies on occasion.

We're not saying to avoid the uncomfortableness of reality; escapism only leads to more heartache down the road. We're saying to become more conscious and self-aware, mindful of how much time and headspace you give to frustrating circumstances—how much of your life you waste dwelling in negativity you can do nothing about. Apply the virtues of temperance and prudence to your life and move forward.

We seldom realize, especially when we're in the thick of the fight, enduring overwhelming stress, or battling tremendous pressure, that our feelings of hopelessness and despair are temporary. That's why knowing how to cultivate consciously a healthy attitude, along with a capable, sound mind, body and spirit, can elevate one to a level of higher thinking and gird us in impenetrable armor. Practicing a positive mindset, choosing hope and happiness over despair, and ultimately realizing your true self will help you resolve situations you didn't know you had the ability to handle.

HOPE: THE ENEMY

To defeat your enemy, you first have to know your enemy. When there is a lack of hope, the following warning signs appear:

- ⊗ **Lack of discipline**; being wasteful with time and resources for want of a goal to work towards; a total lack of work ethic.

- ⊗ **Giving up completely**; succumbing to your inner negative thoughts; self-recrimination and defeatist behavior.

- ⊗ **Anxiety and depression**, particularly with regard to self and one's future; racing thoughts, reacting to stressful situations with panic and frustration.

- ⊗ **Apathy**; a disregard for oneself and others; calling it quits; giving up hope of meeting your day-to-day needs, as well as your lifelong goals and dreams.

- ⊗ **Abandoning all resolve** and anything that resembles perseverance; submitting to the lingering effects of past trauma, including adverse childhood events.

- ⊗ **Making excuses**; acknowledging situations/accidents/life events beyond your control, only to use them as excuses not to progress; giving up any plans for the future in face of something like lingering health concerns.

- ⊗ **Disengaging from the present**; being distracted in the moment by looking to the future or past; being consumed with negative thoughts over what went wrong for you in the past.

X **Blaming yourself for the current set of circumstances**; becoming a victim; using blame and excuses in order to justify your situation; seeking persecution.

X **Victim mentality**; suffering continuously and seeking out others who are just as negative and depressed about their perceived misfortunes as you are.

HOPE: 9-LINE REPORT

We've identified the enemy. What's our plan of action?

1 **Check in:** Understand from the outset that you have more control over your feelings and your destiny than you think. A lack of hope will cloud your vision, while an abundance of hope can take you further than anyone else might think possible.

2 **Identify:** Hope is ethereal, not tangible. However, hope *can* be represented by a tangible item (such as when Benas held Master Gunns' Purple Heart in his hands). Identify tangible signs of hope in your environment that you can use to stir yourself into action.

3 **Prioritize:** What is the nature of the task in front of you, right now? Keep your focus and minimize distractions. Your priority target should be receiving the best of your time and energy.

4 **Make a plan:** Take action, all the while maintaining hope for a positive result. Make the phone calls, gather your resources, get your affairs in order; don't assume success, anticipate it.

5 **Set goals:** What do you want to gain or achieve? In an ideal scenario, where everything goes as well as you hope, what is the outcome?

6 **Commit:** Stand tall. The decision has been made. Don't waver; hesitation is a sign that you aren't staying true to your hopes.

7 **Execute:** Follow through with what you said you were to do, no matter what. It could go wrong, but that doesn't matter. Determine to hope for success even in the face of failure.

8 **Evaluate:** Take a look at how everything turned out, with no regrets. If you did your best and worked for and achieved your goals, you're all the better for it. Let everything you've learned feed your hopes for the future.

9 **Fire for effect:** Live. Learn. Repeat. Each step is a testament to your hope and determination.

HOPE: SIT-REP

- ✓ **Learn to wish for a positive outcome** in your current set of circumstances. Hope is a confident expectation you must take on and embrace as a warrior.

- ✓ **Acknowledge, accept and strengthen your pursuit of perseverance**—the act of doing something when it may be uncomfortable, delaying gratification, or enduring pain in order to reach a desired outcome.

- ✓ **Embrace and practice a positive mind-set.** Understand that there may be a multitude of outcomes, which are unseen in the given moment, but that you have the strength to see things through to the end.

- ✓ **Surround yourself with people who inspire you to be better.** Avoid isolating yourself and stay active. Eliminate those who bring about negativity and waste your precious time.

- ✓ **Involve yourself with peaceful activities that eliminate triggers and stressors.** Consume positive content through activities such as reading, listening to music and watching movies.

- ✓ **Become a practitioner of living life as best you can, allocating your time appropriately.** Make a life-long pursuit of self-care, and choose happiness over despair.

- ✓ **Exercise gratitude.** Be thankful for friends and family, as well as everything you have in life. Verbalize your gratitude. Be mindful of your opportunities, as well as grateful for all that goes right in your personal and professional life.

✔ **Seek professional help when necessary.** Continue to work on overcoming any emotional baggage that has become embedded in your life's programming. Learn to develop a sense of trust.

✔ **When faced with the option of quitting, face things straight on and overcome what you fear**. Recognize that just as negative thoughts are a natural part of life, they go just the same as they come. Recognize them for what they are and let them go.

8

BEARING

"A compliance with the minutiae of military courtesy is a mark of well-disciplined troops."
—MAJOR GENERAL, JOHN A. LEJEUNE, 13TH COMMANDANT OF THE UNITED STATES MARINE CORPS

BEARING IS THE manner in which one carries oneself. Military bearing is possessing or projecting a commanding presence and a professional image of authority. Bearing also describes appropriate behavior: the right demeanor for the right event, at the appropriate time, and in the right place.

BEARING IN THE MARINES

Marine Corps personnel exhibit some of the most recognizable, reassuring and respected public displays of bearing. These are expressions of dignity and honor, and can be seen at military ceremonies, public and private, state funerals and public holiday celebrations (notably Memorial Day and Veteran's Day). Head held high and shoulders back, with a calm, unwavering and intense gaze, coupled with being mentally and physically present in the moment; Marines discipline themselves to curb any visible emotion during any given situation.

A select group of elite U.S. Marines are tasked with guarding all United States embassies around the globe. They are trusted with details of the White House and with the HMX-1 Marine Helicopter Squadron, the fleet of helicopters which escort U.S. presidents and their family members.

ONE OF THE first tests of bearing for Marine recruits reporting to boot camp at Parris Island, South Carolina, comes in the form of the famous yellow footprints awaiting their arrival. As buses roll up in the dead of night, young men and women (often just a few weeks out of high school) sit with their heads down and tucked between their knees. The bus comes to a crawling halt in front of the receiving barracks at Marine Corps Recruit Depot (MCRD). The bus door opens and a Marine Drill Instructor, standing tall in their service Charlie uniform, ascends the steps and centers him or herself in the bus aisle.

The next set of commands are as follows, delivered with a drill instructor's loud and crystal-clear voice:

"Sit up straight! Look at me!"

"FROM THIS POINT ON," the DI says, *"the only words out of your mouth will be 'NO SIR,' 'YES SIR,' AND 'AYE, AYE SIR!'"*

Now that they have the newbies' attention, the drill instructor continues:

"When speaking to a female, you will address them as 'MA'AM.' DO YOU UNDERSTAND?"

The recruits loudly respond: *"Sir, yes, Sir!"* Unable to match the DI's stentorian voice, there is no longer any doubt that the entire group is a motley crew of scared and anxious kids.

"GET OFF MY BUS!" the drill instructor bellows.

"Sir, aye...aye sir!" the bus recruits respond with a pathetic rookie attempt at unison.

They exit the bus with the greatest sense of urgency and fall in, scurrying like startled mice, one person at a time. There they find yellow footprints painted on the asphalt parking lot, each footprint exhibiting the official diagram for the position of attention: heels clicked together at a 45-degree angle, separating the toes and insteps of both feet.

Once all buses are cleared and all footprints are occupied, in exact formation—arm's length from front to back, covered down and perfectly aligned—the recruits are ready for a test of bearing. After the initial contact with the yellow footprints and their drill instructor's reception speech, Parris Island recruits are tested minute-by-minute with initial preparatory commands and disciplined tasks that test their individual bearing and stretch them to greater lengths—lengths many have never experienced.

These tests include the sand fleas that dominate the island, and which can be found crawling all over the recruits' faces; landing inside their ear canals; slipping behind their collar and crawling down their sweaty backs. Hair clippings, left on shoulders and necks after a quick buzz cut, become an irritant as they progress through intense calisthenics. Formation after formation or precision movements, beset on all side by fleas, loose hair and a horde of screaming drill instructors.

But through it all, they learn. They learn that their bearing in formation is as important as their bearing on the rifle range. They learn not to "flag the line," meaning not to point the muzzle of their rifle in a direction for which it is not intended. They learn the discipline expected of Marines, which is necessary for them to focus on their target, maintain their individual body economy, and shoot with precision over long distances. These tests will push them further than they have ever been pushed—all in preparation for combat situations that will push them even further.

BEARING AND PERSONAL APPEARANCE

Marines are expected to exhibit complete control in all tasks performed, both on and off duty. Superior confidence and alertness are always expected and are displayed in one's bearing. How an individual Marine conducts themselves on liberty is just as important as the way he or she behaves and performs in their uniform during training. Marines and warriors must be ready even when others are not.

Another expectation of Marines is to always have a fit, clean body—be clean shaven, clothing pressed, hair kept neat and tidy. This expectation carries over to their weekends and liberty time, as well. A Marine can always be recognized by their clean, crisp shirt tucked in and trousers neatly pressed, usually with a razor-sharp crease down the middle.

To be a warrior, proper hygiene is a prerequisite. A clean body and a professional-looking, well-kept wardrobe are the building blocks for self-respect and bearing. Perception starts to become reality; it's hard for people to take you seriously if they meet you for the first time and you have an unkempt, sloppy appearance.

THE SELECT FEW Marines trusted to contribute to the White House detail are expected never to speak, laugh, fidget or scratch themselves while on post. Their sole responsibility is to open doors and salute selected officials and dignitaries, including the President of the United States. Marines slated for this elite duty understand that there are always cameras and eyes on them, and that they are not to forget those first lessons taught back in boot camp by those menacing drill instructors with eyes in the backs of their heads.

They are to always do the right thing, even when they think no one is watching them. On one windy day at the White House, a Marine standing guard by the West Wing entrance stood stock still without flinching, even when a White House Christmas tree blew over next to him. That bearing was caught on camera, but was done as a matter of course; that is how Marines present themselves to the world. This extension of bearing is expected and executed at every U.S. embassy around the globe, as well as during those special moments such as funeral detail for a fallen warrior, or when a young Marine stands guard with a former U.S. President's casket as it moves about the country towards its intended place of rest.

As with many of the virtues discussed in this book, bearing can seem a bit nebulous; a case of "I'm not sure how it works, but I know it when I see it." Too many people equate bearing with confidence, or with being a sharp dresser, or having a silver tongue. But there's more to it than that, and having a proper bearing means more than just making a good impression.

Bearing is an outward display of inner discipline. It's a combination of factors: how you present yourself to others, the care you take in your appearance, how well you tailor your behavior to a given situation. Having proper bearing inspires trust in others, as well as confidence in oneself. Just wearing a uniform can't do that for you; knowing the right thing to say at the right moment isn't enough. The only way to really cultivate a respectable bearing is to make a commitment to yourself to live up to any and all expectations, personal or otherwise. In doing so, you affirm to yourself and to those around you that you are a person worthy of trust and responsibility.

BEARING: THE ENEMY

To defeat your enemy, you first have to know your enemy. When there is a lack of bearing, the following warning signs appear:

- **Ⓧ** **No perception of one's environment**; no comprehension of the present space and time; dulled senses, tunnel vision; having a negative energy flow.

- **Ⓧ** **Undisciplined behavior and presentation**; directionless and "lost," both physically and mentally; having bad habits, behaviors, emotions and unkempt appearance; poor hygiene, soiled attire that doesn't match the occasion.

- **Ⓧ** **No respect for or awareness of personal and professional space**; not showing recognition of the importance or formality of your setting.

- **Ⓧ** **Negative self-talk**; showing regressed or unhealthful habits.

- **Ⓧ** **Self-centeredness**; not being present for others in the room (including at job interviews and important life events that require your complete mindfulness and presence).

- **Ⓧ** **No thought for your time or the time of others**; appearing restless, anxious; showing no signs of motivation.

- **Ⓧ** **Oversharing**; using others as an excuse to vent personal stories, complaints, and pessimisms that shouldn't be dominant in casual conversations.

❌ Compounding problems, liabilities and debts; failure to course correct and address obvious personal problems, instead going with the flow.

BEARING: 9-LINE REPORT

We've identified the enemy. What's our plan of action?

1 Check-in: This requires an honest self-assessment of your maturity level, tact, and professionalism. Assess timeliness; evaluate the conditions of your immediate environment. In the end, we control our actions, attitudes and feelings. Regardless of the input we receive, we are responsible for and in control of our response to our environment.

2 Identify the issue: Am I being called out for bad behavior? Am I not getting hired, not receiving callbacks after an interview? Sometimes we need to look honestly at where we are and why, as often our behavior is the culprit.

3 Prioritize: Do I want to be an immature child all my life? Or do I want to be successful, respected; to respect myself, and achieve my goals? Know your environment and adjust your behavior accordingly. Pursue excellence in action. A lack of bearing where it's called for, or unacceptable and unfiltered behavior in general, can be a sign of a bigger problem. Acting like the class clown in *every* environment, at work and at play, at the office and at happy hour, can be a sign of poor self-esteem or personal insecurities. Seeking professional help or finding a mentor can assist in identifying these roadblocks.

4 Make a plan: Face reality. If you're not ready, acknowledge it. But be honest and don't compromise your own goals or inhibit the goals of those around you. Don't be the one that brings the ship down.

5 **Set goals:** You have the option of setting high standards for yourself, such that each day leaves you a better person than you were before. Or, you can waste your entire life partying, to the detriment of your self and those around you. Regardless of which you choose, that goal will determine your actions going forward. Do yourself a favor and make the *right* choice.

6 **Commit:** Once you decide to work on improving your bearing, do what needs to be done to get better at it. Do your research; take into account the suggestions in this book. Things tend to work out when you apply what you've learned.

7 **Execute:** Anything can look good on paper. Paper is the home of perfect, foolproof plans. The real test comes from putting yourself in vulnerable positions and having the fortitude to maintain your bearing in a stressful environment. If you don't know what is appropriate, go back a few steps and *identify the issue* again.

8 **Evaluate:** Assess your improvement. Are others around you noticing and commenting on your positive changes? *Are people taking me more seriously, or am I still stuck at the kiddie table during holiday meals?*

9 **Fire for effect:** If all things point to positivity, you've improved your bearing. Keep going and take the time to check in with trusted friends on what you're doing right and where you can still improve.

BEARING: SIT-REP

√ **When excuses and distractions slip in, engage yourself in action**—to an extreme, if necessary—to correct the issue and regain focus.

√ **Show yourself respect by dressing to impress**. Wear clothing that is comfortable, form-fitting and neatly pressed. You *will* start to feel better about yourself. Attention to detail with your attire, hygiene and physical fitness is what will place you on the path to becoming a warrior elite.

√ **Incorporate activities, places and events into your life that require your best, most professional behavior**. Proper diet, nutrition and fitness are a regular part of the warrior lifestyle.

√ **Create areas in your life that incorporate more discipline and structure in your daily schedule**. Start by having a set time you wake up, eat your meals, journal, exercise, iron your work clothes, prep your healthy lunches, etc.

√ **Be aware of how others see you.** Perception is often reality; how others perceive you and your current behaviors will set the tone for your working relationship. Make sure they reflect positively on you. Giving yourself the opportunity to shine and succeed will embolden you for the future. Understand that there are always eyes on you, smartphone cameras at the ready to archive any misstep—or good deed. Always maintain a neat, clean and highly pressed presence.

- **Make better use of your time.** Read more books and learn new things in order to introduce novelty into your life. The results of this type of self-cultivation can only help in those ultimate tests of bearing.

- **Cultivate situational awareness in all areas of life**. Look in all directions, including looking up and looking down. Maintain a professional bearing in any and all environments; there shouldn't be "cheat days" for the way you present yourself to the world.

9

JUSTICE

"At his best, man is the noblest of all animals. Separated from law and justice he is his worst."
—ARISTOTLE

JUSTICE IS THE practice of maintaining or working towards what is right, fair and equal. In some respects it is the most important of the Cardinal Virtues, because it is justice that regulates and maintains humanity's connections with each other.

In practice, justice is being genuine, true and fair; having and showing respect for self and others. With its roots in Greek philosophy of how individuals and societies should act, justice is the foundation of what we understand to be the rule of law.

Everyday justice means doing the right thing, in matters large and small. When we do our best with the tools at our disposal, and achieve the optimum outcome, that's justice. To earn something positive, to achieve our goals and accomplish great works can only be the result of making right decisions. Achieving greatness through hard work is most often the result for doing the right thing.

When hard work yields abundance, that is a mark of justice. Even doing small, simple things every day involves making right and just decisions. These are opportunities to build solid habits and sharpen our capabilities for overcoming obstacles. If we strive for justice, the issues we encounter later in life, though they may be larger in scale, will pose no challenge to us, confident in the knowledge that practicing justice will reap equally large rewards.

We achieve justice and fuel our own greatness by continually moving forward. Strive to make your decisions fearlessly, always visualizing a positive outcome. That being said, justice should not be confused with entitlement. Just because you think you deserve something, or feel justified in the pursuit of something, it doesn't mean your failure to achieve it constitutes a failure of justice. Humans aren't always right, but justice is.

IF BUZZ'S LEADERSHIP had had its way, he would have been stuck behind a naval desk somewhere for the entirety of his term. But for Buzz, the thought of his Marines deploying without him was completely out of the question—he could not even fathom the idea. Buzz knew in the deepest depths of his soul deploying was the right thing to do—his men needed him on the ground, and he knew best how to do his job properly.

There was never any doubt in his mind...though there was plenty in the minds of the higher-ups. The process went on for months, with Buzz fighting tooth and nail to deploy. He was told, "No." He persisted; they told him, "NO." This became a not-so-private campaign, as commanding officers told him many times over that he would be staying back, that they needed Navy corpsmen stateside, the end.

But Buzz continued to push back, seeking every available channel to plead his case. His outright defiance of the powers-that-be wasn't because he was trying to be difficult, or that he was acting like a petulant child; but he was going with his men, period. They needed him. There was justice to be had. He wasn't going to stay stateside and work behind a desk, for the only reason that mattered: because he knew it was the right thing to do.

CULTIVATING PERSONAL JUSTICE

When we understand justice as "right action," figuring out how to cultivate justice in our personal life seems pretty straightforward. To a certain extent, we can rely on our conscience to see us through; we know not to harm someone without reason or provocation, we know to keep our promises, we know to tip our servers.

Where it gets a bit trickier is when it comes to observing justice in our personal life towards *ourselves.* While the world doesn't owe us a thing—hard though that may be to hear—there's quite a bit that we owe ourselves, and we're not always good about doing so. We owe ourselves proper sleep and nutrition; we owe ourselves some sort of recreation and socialization; we owe ourselves opportunities to learn, grow and develop—to meet new challenges and overcome them.

It's easy to say that we want to do the right thing, but all too often we "treat" ourselves or give ourselves a pass instead of doing the right thing. We drop hundreds of dollars on things we want instead of saving up for the things we need. We gorge on junk food and binge watch television instead of going for a walk or reading a book.

You deserve better. Your physical, mental and emotional health are your responsibility, and when you abandon that responsibility you are committing an injustice against yourself.

As for how to cultivate this type of justice in your life: if you're still not sure, go back and re-read the last eight chapters! Self-discipline, careful prudence, temperance and moderation—practicing any and all of these virtues better prepares you to listen to that little voice in your head that's telling you what to do (and not do).

Don't give yourself excuses, and don't try to get yourself off on a technicality. Nobody's buying it, least of all you—so let's get to work.

PLATO'S JUSTICE

During his lifetime, the Greek philosopher Plato was witness to numerous acts of injustice, not the least of which was the death of his teacher Socrates. A passionate critic of the state of affairs in Athens at the time, Socrates was found guilty on trumped up charges of impiety and corrupting the minds of the youth and sentenced to death.

Plato shared Socrates' unfavorable view of Athens and its people, citing excessive individualism and a lack of cohesion as chief among their failures—failures which had led to their recent defeat by Sparta and the subsequent near-collapse of their democratic system as rich and poor became increasingly divided and social cooperation became non-existent. (You don't have to look hard to find certain similarities between the Athens of Plato's day and the polarized state of modern America.)

In his search for a solution to these societal ills, Plato turned his attention to reimagining the concept of justice. Rather than the law of the land, which had seen his teacher executed just to silence him, Plato argued for a sort of justice that had not yet been seen in Greece. While his contemporaries argued that justice meant practicing good conduct in all things, or seeing to it that everyone receives what they are due, Plato disagreed. To his way of thinking, justice was not a simple balancing of the books, or a power given to the courts to keep order in the streets. Instead, justice should be thought of as something internal—as a virtue of the individual, rather than a part of society as a whole.

Eventually, Plato published his thoughts in his *Republic*, in which he outlined his idea of justice as being the virtue of man that makes us not only good, but self-consistent. A just person is one who works to the betterment of himself and his society in all things: "Man should practice one thing only and that the thing to which his nature was best adopted."

Plato's ideal society was one in which every person worked to be the best person they could be, both for the sake of themselves and for those around them. Justice was not a question of reward and punishment, or even of right and wrong; it was a question of maintaining individual and social harmony, for the betterment of all.

Plato's ideas of justice aren't quite practical in the modern age—with over 300,000,000 people living in America at time of writing, there's a need for some sort of organized system of justice to keep things running smoothly. But these systems are intended to serve as oversight—you can't just write down a list of rules and think you've captured the entirety of justice.

True justice is tied to the individual; Plato was dead on in that respect. We understand justice through the lens of our conscience, and feel it is best demonstrated by taking righteous action. Be true to yourself. Be fair with others. Do the right thing. Be confident and accept the consequences of any and all choices you make. Respect for yourself and respect from others will follow.

This is the definition of justice.

JUSTICE: THE ENEMY

To defeat your enemy, you first have to know your enemy. When there is a lack of justice, the following warning signs appear:

- **Acting belligerently**; practicing criminal behavior; acting out and exhibiting unjust characteristic traits; those not found in warriors.

- **Inequity**; evil and unfair acts; favoritism.

- **Disservice**; doing wrong by others; expecting fast promotions, more pay, unlimited opportunities and benefits in your career without putting in the work.

- **Dishonesty**; not being true to yourself or others; dishonor.

- **Acting selfishly** in the performance of your duties, not placing group welfare or customer service as your top priority; being self-entitled.

- **Pursuing goals in life in a faithless or half-hearted manner**, making poor decisions every step of the way; making irrational decisions.

- **Having no respect for yourself or others**; exhibiting selfish and regressed behaviors as an adult.

- **Succumbing to fear and an actionless lifestyle design**; giving in to the ideas, thoughts and suggestions of colleagues, friends and family; living out their unjust idea of you.

JUSTICE: 9-LINE REPORT

We've identified the enemy. What's our plan of action?

1 Check in: Read the situation and determine your responsibilities towards the parties involved. Is justice being served? Ignored? Is this a situation where your help would be welcome? Necessary?

2 Identify: What role are you being called to play in this situation? Are you the plaintiff, with a responsibility to clearly and decisively plead your case? Are you the defendant, responsible for making sure your voice is heard? Are you the judge, with final say on whether justice is served?

3 Prioritize: In prioritizing tasks, pay close attention to whether this situation truly concerns you. If your actions as an outside party will only serve to muddy the water, then your priorities should be elsewhere.

4 Make a plan: When determining the best course of action, remember to evaluate pros and cons where applicable. In many cases, several involved parties may have legitimate claims and arguments; you'll need to make sure nothing gets lost in the shuffle due to poor planning.

5 Set goals: Identify what each party, yourself included, is hoping for as an outcome. Does everyone seek a fair and equitable resolution to the conflict?

6 Commit: Once you insert yourself into the situation, you're in there all the way. Don't unnecessarily complicate things by stirring up the hornet's nest and then leaving right away; see things through to the end.

⑦ **Execute:** Take action. Once a decision has been reached, put it into practice and see how things go. It might just provide everyone with the opportunity to move forward.

⑧ **Evaluate:** Were your actions helpful? Justified? What were the results?

⑨ **Fire for effect:** Live. Learn. Repeat. If another problem occurred as a result of your actions, recall the earlier steps: stay committed, redouble your efforts, start from the top and try again.

JUSTICE: SIT-REP

√ **Take the time to do some soul searching.** Create a list of aspirations, dreams and hopes. Taking time to complete an internal inventory (asking questions like, "What do I like," "What do I dislike," "What drives me," "Who do I want to be as a person") allows a person to take ownership of their life. These moments of introspection can help a person to better know themselves.

√ **Don't cheat yourself.** Honesty is important. Know yourself and stay true to yourself; remain unconcerned with the actions, behaviors and opinions of others.

√ **Be authentic, be decisive, and take confident action.** Taking action is crucial and must include sound moral judgement and discretion. Being reckless and impulsive leads to bad decisions. Follow your conscience.

√ **Be humble.** When necessary, take a moment to examine yourself as from the outside looking in, and embrace humility. Eliminate grandiose expectations and self-entitlement.

√ **Eliminate irrational decision-making.** So many mistakes are made, so many injustices allowed, not by cruelty but by carelessness.

√ **Always be fair in your doings, even with those you feel don't deserve it.** All people deserve justice. Determine to identify any selfish and regressed behaviors in your life and root them out. Stop blaming others and take ownership of any shortcomings or failures.

● **Don't succumb to fear, creating an actionless lifestyle design**. Take charge of your life and start moving forward, even if it's just one step at a time.

10

FAITH

"It's been taught that your worst enemy couldn't harm you as much as your own wicked thoughts."
—WU TANG CLAN

"We've backed off in good faith to try and give you a chance to straighten this problem out. But I'm going to beg with you for a minute. I'm going to plead with you, do not cross us. Because if you do, the survivors will write about what we do here for 10,000 years."
—GENERAL JAMES MATTIS

FAITH IS A virtue that binds humanity together. It unites people, even during the darkest and worst of times, as well as during the brightest, best of times. Faith is often referred to as trust without reservation, and it can materialize at the most unexpected times. It can take the form of a sense of trust and confidence in others; it can be a belief in a higher power, the confidence that there is a reason for everything. Faith is the intuitive conviction that you are doing the right thing, and that good will prevail.

We don't always have a firm concept we can definitively point to that proves faith works; like many of the virtues, it's an abstract concept. Faith doesn't have a physical surface we can touch; it's unseen, we *feel* it. Poet and writer Luci Shaw explains: "Faith and love, perfect or imperfect, are intangibles—we experience them but cannot quite put our finger on or define them; they seem to escape us. Such spiritual qualities are, by definition, 'unseen.' We move in their direction, hopeful, believing, but seldom achieving with absolute certainty."

Faith is what holds together religions and business groups, sports teams and military units, friends and families. Faith connects us in grief, the universal condition we all experience in times of loss. But faith binds humanity in times of joy, as well. Faith is what brings a warrior through a battle. With faith, those fighting have a framework of established trust and confidence in the warrior on their right and left, knowing they will battle on, enjoying the small victories and appreciating what they have in the moment. With faith, courage and strength excel. Warriors have mastered these character attributes, honed them with life experience.

When faith is absent, we see ourselves become morally unmoored, especially in times of deep distress. It's no secret that the world is becoming more polarized, and one of the overarching themes in present day society is that people are on their own. People operate under the guise of independence, but that supposed freedom is false; it only conceals unfortunate behaviors and attitudes of false entitlement, goals influenced by instant gratification, overreaching expectations of unearned respect, and a disrespect for those with more life experience.

Many living in contemporary society lack an internal compass. We act impulsively, with complete and total disregard for others. These people are the furthest thing from warriors; they want the bright and shiny things in life, working from selfish ulterior motives. Always looking for the quickest route to the most gain, regardless of whether it's deserved, they are without plans and without support. Directionless and lost, they offer a grim look at what a future without faith looks like.

———

AT ONE POINT, Buzz worked with Casualty Assistance Calls Officers (CACO) under the direction of the secretary of the U.S. Navy. In this position, he was tasked with delivering notifications to families and loved ones in the event of a casualty. It was a necessary task; sobering and serious, it required a responsible, respectable person.

Buzz stepped up and showed up. Officers often had limited information concerning the circumstances of the casualty or injury when they showed up on someone's doorstep. Sometimes he'd have to inform multiple families on the same day for the same individual (usually due to separation and/or divorce). It's an intense experience for CACOs; emotionally draining for the officers, they are nevertheless taking on the obligation, a job responsibility with no room for error, of telling a family that their son, daughter, brother, sister or spouse has either been killed or gravely injured.

Goes without saying it's no picnic for the families and loved ones on the receiving end, either.

Buzz knew he had to be ready for any reaction, however raw. He remembers a woman getting out of her car who took one look at him standing on the sidewalk, dressed in full military attire, turned on her heel and took off in the opposite direction.

Any unpredictably raw and emotive reaction from a person is possible. Both sides are under extreme stress in the moment, physically and mentally; anything can happen, and CACOs are called upon to be ready. Yet as hard a job as it was (and continues to be for those who do it), Buzz and the other CACOs were further constrained by the amount of information they could share; the questions they could—and could not—answer. All while not inflicting any more pain on the family members and loved ones than necessary.

No small feat.

There is one family visit in particular which sticks out in Buzz's memory, which speaks to the strong character and goodness of the people involved. As Buzz tells it, the 21-year-old reported KIA was a 6 foot, 4-inch-tall imposing hulk of a Marine. While notifying loved ones is intended to be done as soon as possible, the reality of the situation tends to be a bit slower. As it tends to go sometimes on a military clock, with people just doing their jobs and getting their ducks in a row, Buzz and his colleagues were delayed in conducting the notification.

Finally, at 10:30 pm (on the same day the Marine in question was blown up by an IED), the CACOs make their presence known on the family's doorstep. The father of the Marine killed in action answered the door, and to this day Buzz remains in awe of the man. In Buzz' own words: "The father had to know why we were there...and the first words out of his mouth were, 'My God. You guys have a difficult job.'"

The father didn't yet know that his son was killed, and wasn't coming back. Yet Buzz knew, as soon as the father spoke, that this man's generous, forgiving words— spoken in his darkest hour—came from a place of extraordinary heart. The qualities that define the virtues of bearing, discipline, hope and faith know no bounds, even in moments like this. By showing utterly selfless concern for the CACOs, the Marine's father exhibited an extraordinary bearing at one of the most awful moments of his life. Buzz, himself a father, remembers the man's stature at this agonizing moment, as something to be forever respected, emanating unusual faith, considering the circumstances, but which was immediately recognized—and overwhelmingly appreciated.

CULTIVATING FAITH

It might be said that faith can't be trusted until it has been tested. For some, when that test comes and they find their faith isn't up to the task, the result is that they become lost. Maybe they find themselves worn down by a long fight with a terminal illness, or stunned into disbelief by a sudden loss of a job, a home, a loved one. They try to rely on their faith, religious or otherwise, that the bad times will pass…but time goes on and there's still no end in sight.

What is missing from this scenario is the most important component of faith: *action*. As with every virtue we've discussed in this book, in the end everything comes down to how you act and what you do. Faith does not mean trusting that the universe won't let you slip through the cracks; the world we live in is too harsh for that. What it means is taking a step forward while having faith that you'll be able to catch yourself if you fall.

So, how do you cultivate this type of "active faith?" Perseverance and fortitude both play a role, as you might expect. If you've weathered the bad times, and you've strengthened your resolve to move through those bad times, you're already in a great position. If you haven't, perhaps it's time to rely on charity. There's nothing wrong with relying on those around you to offer a hand as you pick yourself up and dust yourself off—especially when they know you'd do the same for them. Asking for help when you need it is another great way to practice active faith, by having faith in others.

And finally, practice temperance. It's all well and good to want to pick yourself up by your bootstraps and move forward, confident in your ability to succeed. But not every battle is a one-and-done; sometimes you need to settle in for a long, protracted struggle where there truly *is* no end in sight. The worst things in life aren't always over quickly, and you need to know to pace yourself, taking each day one step at a time, practicing proper self-care and staying as strong as you can. Just put your head down, keep pushing forward, and have faith that there *is* something better waiting for you. The only thing that's certain: if you stop where you are, paralyzed in placed, things are never going to get better.

THE SETTING WAS *Fallujah in wartime, 2004. Half the buildings had been blown to smithereens, and every structure had a hole in it. Not exactly high on the annual list of top vacation destinations at the time.*

It was pitch black out, and spooky. Units in charge of clearing the buildings set up strobe lights at night to indicate buildings had been cleared, with the unintended result that strobe lights would throw out random, fleeting shadows that tricked the mind into seeing movement, danger and the general unknown. Adding to the city's charm, the streets had been deliberately flooded by enemy forces in an effort to thwart transportation—a complete failure, as Humvees have no problem with flood waters—but all electricity had been cut.

During the invasion, the situation was fluid and constantly evolving; circumstances were prone to change in an instant. Situational intelligence was often unavailable or inaccurate. One night mission in particular called for extracting prisoners and moving them to Abu Ghraib prison. The convoy of four Humvees entered the city having been given coordinates to their destination, only to find their directions were to "turn left" into a large hole in the wall...after a hole in the wall.

This instruction did not refer to a cheap restaurant with great Mexican food; it didn't even mean a dive bar with happy hour at 1600. It meant a literal hole in the wall. That was it. That was all they had to go on.

It took Bloom and the unit four approaches, but eventually they found their location and achieved their mission. Bloom attributes their success to faith; a faith that there existed something or someone bigger than them who was guiding them. Bloom put faith in their directions, in their military training and in themselves. Secure in the knowledge that they weren't being led into an untenable situation, or a situation they couldn't handle, they persevered in their mission and achieved success as a result.

Faith in yourself. Faith in your comrades. Faith in your leaders. Faith in your cause.

Faith takes many forms, but they all serve the same purpose. They all provide a unique kind of support, where no one and nothing else can. The willingness to embrace the best-case scenario in the name of moving forward is what has kept humanity going all these years, as we work to turn our faith into reality. It isn't always easy—nothing worthwhile ever is—but we wouldn't get anywhere without it.

Faith is counted as one of what's known as the three Theological Virtues; the other two are hope and love (sometimes called charity). Of the three, faith is perhaps the easiest to overlook, as hope and love continue to drive us forward towards our goals. Yet faith is no less important: without the ability to have faith in another person, love is impossible, and without faith in ourselves and those around us, hope is meaningless. It is faith which provides us with the inner strength necessary to realize our hopes and improve ourselves. Where all else fails, faith endures.

Semper Fi. *Always* Faithful.

FAITH: THE ENEMY

To defeat your enemy, you first have to know your enemy. When there is a lack of faith, the following warning signs appear:

- **Dwelling on regrets and past mistakes**, instead of looking for ways forward; exhibiting depression about past events.

- **A lack of trust**; having no confidence in yourself or others.

- **Lack of hope**, especially in oneself; exhibiting anxiety about future events.

- **Making big problems out of little problems**, or compounding existing issues together to create more difficulty.

- **Not believing in "the mission," whatever that may be**; being selfish; ignoring the needs of others.

- **Longing for instant gratification**; submitting to your addictions; relapsing or backsliding into old negative behaviors.

- **Disdain for preparing and training**; an absence of motivation due to an expectation of failure.

- **A penchant for hatred and violence** stemming from a fear of understanding.

FAITH: 9-LINE REPORT

We've identified the enemy. What's our plan of action?

1 **Check in:** Having a lack of faith, whether in yourself, your situation, or those around you, can cloud your vision. Assess whether you can accurately read the room, and if necessary, ask for a second opinion.

2 **Identify:** Just like hope, faith isn't something you can see or touch, but it makes its presence known in tangible ways—the people around you, the resources you have access to, etc. Identify the advantages you already have, and believe that you'll be able to come up with a plan that uses them to their fullest extent.

3 **Prioritize:** Determine exactly what areas of the situation you have control over, and to what extent. Everything else—those elements that are completely out of your control—leave to faith. Even if you have no other options available, don't be held back by lack of faith.

4 **Make a plan:** When we make plans, we rely on our skills, our companions, and the tools we have available. We have faith our skills are up to the task, our companions have our backs, and our tools won't break down.

5 **Set goals:** Envision the ideal outcome for your scenario. Picture it in your mind, and make the choice to work towards it no matter what. Unexpected situations may arise; have faith that your training and planning will see you through.

⑥ **Commit:** Faith pays out what you put in. Give everyone around you one more reason to have faith in your judgment and your skill. Stand tall.

⑦ **Execute:** Put the plan into motion. Have faith in the process, and everything you've brought to bear.

⑧ **Evaluate:** Have no regrets. Pass or fail, victory or defeat, what was left in your hands has been accounted for, what was left out of your hands is out of your control.

⑨ **Fire for effect:** Live. Learn. Repeat. A single victory proves nothing, and neither does a single failure. Regardless of the outcome, have faith in yourself, and in the knowledge that you can *always* do better next time.

FAITH: SIT-REP

- ✅ **Have trust in your abilities and learn how to entrust yourself to others**. Work on developing yourself in order to build up your confidence and self-esteem. Develop mindfulness and good thoughts.

- ✅ **Delay instant gratification**. If you still want something in two weeks, you can start assessing how best to obtain it. Express gratitude for the things and the loved ones you have in your life.

- ✅ **Stop valuing others' opinions over your own**, or to the exclusion of all other standards of self-evaluation.

- ✅ **Resolve to keep believing in the vision of your trusted leaders, and in the mission you've started.** Understand that strength and resilience will be needed for the difficulties that lie ahead, while knowing that you have the potential to achieve both.

- ✅ **Learn to look at the bigger picture**. You may not always understand it but taking a long look at the world around you can really put your problems in perspective. Acknowledge and address the issues and conditions that interfere with your daily life. Consider seeking professional help and support for your addictions.

- ✅ **Avoid regrets by making decisions confidently**, having enough faith in yourself to trust your own judgment. Trust yourself and others; eliminate anxiety about the future or depression about the past by staying strong in the present.

● **Remove the tendency towards instant gratification.** When hard work and long-term rewards are absent, faith appears less necessary, a mindset that can only lead to future disappointment and stagnation.

● **Get treatment for your addictions.** Treat relapses and negative behaviors as obstacles to overcome, not as personal failings. By doing so, you learn to trust your own competence.

● **Avoid selfishness.** Tend to the needs of others when you have the time and resources, and you will come to appreciate how much good will and support the world really contains.

11

RESILIENCE

"My barn having burned down, I can now see the moon."
—MIZUTA MASAHIDE, 17TH CENTURY JAPA-
NESE POET AND SAMURAI

RESILIENCE IS TRICKY to define. Unlike charity, which can be seen in the effect it has on those who receive it, or fortitude and decisiveness, which can be observed in how a person performs under pressure, resilience is much more subtle. Similar to temperance, resilience is a quiet, underlying trait; a strength which sits below the surface. Resilience is marked by what you *don't* see, rather than what you do: if you don't see a person giving up or giving in, if you don't see a person compromising on their principles to make something easier, if you don't see a person taking the quick and dirty way out—that's resilience at work.

Resiliency is a state of mind, a way of life. More than that, it's a multi-level approach to problem solving, one which is made up all of the virtues we've discussed. To give a slightly more concrete explanation, resiliency can also be described as resolve. The word resolve featured heavily in the rhetoric of President George W. Bush after the attacks on September 11, 2001, in which he proclaimed that America's resolve would be swift and just. That no institution, nation, person or terrorist network would be able to break down our resolve as they had the twin towers. Our resolve would become unwavering.

The actions that took place in the days and years that followed show not only the determination of our military, but also how dedicated our society was to freedom and justice. The opportunity to embrace a "woe is me" attitude after 9/11 was right there, but it didn't find any takers, because we understood that our resiliency was being tested—and we knew what needed to be done to move forward.

RESILIENCE IN THE FACE OF ADVERSITY

Most of us are apprehensive when faced with large decisions. We fear the possibility of making a mistake, of being called to the carpet to answer for an oversight or error that is our sole responsibility. Sadly, this fear keeps many of us from taking on those types of responsibilities; or worse, keeps us from taking ownership of the error. Instead, we try to play things off or deflect blame, concerned only with saving face or downplaying the circumstances because we have a reputation to maintain.

But for all that this *might* help us save face in the short term, the only thing this type of avoidance truly reinforces is our weakness to rebound successfully. Regardless of how good a spin job we put on a mistake after the fact, it still raises questions about our integrity among those around us. They see how we don't have the intestinal fortitude to take ownership of our mistake, and as a result will think twice in the future about trusting us with anything important.

But what is arguably worse is what this does to your own self-image. When faced with a situation where you have the option of either sucking it up, taking your lumps and standing up for yourself, or bowing out, running and hiding, our choice informs how much faith we'll have in ourselves going forward. Self-esteem is like a bank account; we're either making deposits or withdrawals, and with each withdrawal, both from the bank and the situation at hand, we come closer to going broke.

The best response is to own it. The quickest way to make improvements in our lives is to immediately own up to and identify our shortcomings when they hit us in the face. When we admit to such things, the learning process has already begun and we enable ourselves to recover soundly from adversity.

This process requires being brutally honest with ourselves. We've all heard stories or personally experienced someone being brutally honest with us, and while at times it stings or ruins relationships, if we don't have an honest view of ourselves, then there is no way we can be successful. Words can sting, they can hurt, but if we are completely honest in our own assessment, then they can never be more than words. They can't dictate to us how we lead our lives. Be open to what others are saying, but resolve to always be your own harshest critic.

BUILDING RESILIENCE

In order to remain resilient, we must always see to our basic, essential needs. Nothing solid can be built on a crumbling foundation. To that end, it's helpful to consider the model suggested by the American psychologist Abraham Maslow, in his paper *A Theory of Human Motivation*. Known as Maslow's hierarchy of needs, this model arranges the five categories of basic human requirements for health and happiness into a pyramid, with each subsequent level building on what has come before.

These are:

1. Physiological needs

2. Safety

3. Love/belonging

4. Esteem

5. Self-actualization

As a warrior, the physiological needs are often the most pressing. You need to be able to breathe, hydrate yourself with fresh, clean water, and eat healthy and nutritious food. Adequate rest and sleep are also required. Safety comes directly afterwards, covering shelter from the elements and protection from most danger and fear. Social needs, referred to above as "Love/belonging," require you to have a sense that you are accepted in your environment, respected and wanted. This is natural; as warriors, we need to be validated, valued, accepted and respected. We want to be able to take pride in our personal passions and pursuits. This outward support translates to inner strength, as we build self-esteem, a source of energy and strength that we can call upon when times get tough.

And it all builds towards the top of Maslow's pyramid, self-actualization: an ongoing process for every warrior, but one which we can only succeed at through perseverance and resilience. If you're finding your resolve starting to slip, it might be helpful to do a self-assessment with Maslow's hierarchy in mind. If you don't feel you're standing on solid ground, look to your basic needs and see if they're really being fulfilled. If not, start trying to build yourself up in simple, practical ways, and just see how much stronger you feel.

Nobody makes it through this wonderful journey we call life without facing adversity, getting beat up and knocked around. "Semper Fidelis," or "Always Faithful," has long been a mantra of the Marine Corps. And while it has a lot of applications, take it here to mean that you should always be able to have faith in your own personal strength. No one has more opportunities to have your back than you. And if the idea of resilience still seems a bit unclear, here's the takeaway: don't quit. Let your response to tough times be swift and direct, and don't let your enthusiasm burn out as you strive towards the goals you've set for yourself. Enjoy the ride: it's bumpy as hell, but so worth it!

RESILIENCE: THE ENEMY

To defeat your enemy, you first have to know your enemy. When there is a lack of resilience, the following warning signs appear:

- **Feelings of helplessness**; a fear of failure or success.

- **Taking advantage of parents or friends**; using them as a crutch or financial support system throughout adulthood.

- **Lack of growth** in your personal and professional life; lack of a passionate role in your career.

- **No self-actualization**; lack of strong identity.

- **Isolating from friends, family and co-workers**; a feeling of not belonging to a community; being adrift.

- **Neglecting your physical, mental and spiritual health**; ignoring long-standing symptoms of anxiety and depression (until there's a problem).

- **Lack of follow-through** in communications with others; lack of professionalism; frequently changing careers or employers.

- **Financial illiteracy; increasing debt, lack of assets**; failure to take advantage of prior education and work experience.

RESILIENCE: 9-LINE REPORT

We've identified the enemy. What's our plan of action?

1 Check in: If you've made it this far, then you've already exhibited resilience. Putting in the work to achieve your goals and attain your aspirations proves your resilience. Feelings of entitlement will most certainly *not* get you there. The world owes you nothing, and gives no favors. You will get beat up, kicked around, and knocked down during this journey.

2 Identify: Fear of the unknown, fear of failure, fear of not fitting in; these are real issues in today's society. You are not alone. But only *you* can identify and act on what is holding you back from obtaining greatness. There is no application for "Greatness" that you can fill out and drop off at the post office. Greatness has to be earned.

3 Prioritize: Issues with resiliency usually mirror the absence of one or more of the virtues we've discussed up to this point. Taking the time and energy to make yourself better each day in these areas will build individual resiliency.

4 Make a plan: Avoid becoming overwhelmed, and finish what you start. This is the core of resilience. Failing once is not the universe telling you to quit; in fact, failure is often a necessary part of the journey. Get back up and keep going. That said, remember that there's a fine line between persistence and insanity. Know when to adjust and re-direct. It's a delicate balance, but listen to your gut and take your environment into account.

⑤ Set goals: The first step to avoiding failure is making realistic goals. Each step forward, no matter how small, makes the next step that much easier. Stay practical, respect your abilities as well as your limits, and success will follow.

⑥ Commit: Resiliency *is* commitment—the two go hand-in-hand. But what you practice in small ways each day will be mirrored in big ways in your life as a whole. Stay committed to yourself, to your friends and family, to your professional obligations. Treat failure not as a setback but as a lesson. Having this mindset keeps you committed, regardless of the situation.

⑦ Execute: As you move forward with a given plan, be prepared for failure. Failure is never the goal, but it *is* going to happen. Have a backup plan—maybe more than one. If you commit to greatness, you will use them.

⑧ Evaluate: Take an internal inventory. Our dreams are not always in line with our reality, and being resilient in all the wrong areas is not productive. Be aware that goals may need to be adjusted, or completely changed. Make the necessary adjustments or outright changes and keep going.

⑨ Fire for effect: Mission complete. You've either experienced success, or you've experienced failure. Regardless of which, take pride in your effort. You've come a long way to experience a sense of achievement and accomplishment, and whether you've crossed the finish line or you've got further to go, there's no way left but forward.

RESILIENCE: SIT-REP

✅ **Celebrate your small victories**. Face success and build upon it. Face failure and embrace it as a learning experience, a moment of growth.

✅ **Replace feelings of hopelessness with massive amounts of action**. Be passionate about your current situation, regardless of whether it's a temp job or a professional career. Make growth in your personal and professional life a requisite part of your plan.

✅ **Don't use your parents as a crutch or a financial support system throughout your adulthood**. Stop asking to borrow money from friends and colleagues. Improve your financial literacy and gain a better hold on your spending.

✅ **Adopt transparency in everything you do and expect the same from others**. Take care in your communication with others to be professional and responsive.

✅ **Don't isolate from your friends, family and co-workers**. Make an effort to fit in with your local community. By engaging with the world around you, you gain a better sense of your place within it; these connections will strengthen you during hard times.

✅ **Care for your physical, mental and spiritual health**. Address any long-term problems by seeing a professional, if necessary.

☑ **If a job is getting tough, stick it out**. Finish the tasks in front of you, even as you look for new and better opportunities.

☑ **Step up and maximize your education and previous work experience**. Take full advantage of your ultimate potential.

Conclusion

A T TIME OF writing, the world has just celebrated the 100th anniversary of the end of World War I. At the eleventh hour of 11/11/1918, an armistice—effectively a truce—was signed to end hostilities on the Western Front of World War I. "The war to end all wars," named as such by those who hoped and believed militarism could be eliminated from humanity's landscape, World War I remains one the deadliest conflicts in the history of the human race. Globally significant wars have since dashed the hopes of those who sat down to peace talks that November day in 1918—humanity continues to see and experience battles where both virtue and vice are fully on display, borne out through skirmishes and victories, as well as costly defeats.

In 1919, the first Armistice Day was celebrated in the United States with small town parades and speeches by veteran officers and politicians of their time, honoring those warriors who came home to march in these parades. It's humbling to note that just a century ago—a short amount of time considering the longevity of the Four Cardinal Virtues—these concepts thrived in times of peace and war both, just as they do now. Bearing, honor, courage, endurance, sacrifice, unselfishness, loyalty…the rich soil of virtue gave life to these concepts and others as they threaded throughout the history books.

The virtues have a staying power that overcomes time and space. 100 years is just a flash in the cosmos, by comparison.

Virtues are the building blocks of character. By their nature, warriors are expected to lead with virtue. Warriors who have honed their characters exist in every era, in every century, every decade, every day—in military conflict, in governance, on our streets and in our homes.

Because virtue is like the warrior: it fights, too. Virtue doesn't give up. Virtue inspires strategy and executes on preparation. Virtue fights injustice, it defeats cowardice, it battles impulsiveness, conflict and greed; it reins in selfishness, inequity, self-destructiveness and vice.

Virtue fights for what's right.

Humanity's inherent capacity for good and evil endures, as well. Indomitable warriors, those military-trained alongside the everyday man and woman, with hearts full of ambitious conscience and a desire for good, happy endings and a better life, continue to throw themselves into the competitions, the battles, the fights and the skirmishes.

The virtues have existed for thousands of years, seen thousands of peaceful, starry nights—and their legacy has endured. Perhaps the good embedded in us can win out over time.

There is no guidebook that can help you solve every situation in life. Sometimes you will have to choose virtue over vice in order to adapt and overcome a situation. But regardless, warriors must always accept full responsibility for their actions. Virtue is what strengthens a warrior; a warrior with strong virtues, mindfulness, stable mental health, and superior physical fitness develops desirable qualities that reward continuously.

Embracing adaptability and flexibility enables the warrior to adjust, even in these rapidly changing times. It's important to adopt new tactics and techniques, take in new information, reorganize and become more efficient to succeed in an ever-changing environment. Become a practitioner of virtue and start practicing now in order to be prepared when it counts. This will allow you to quickly locate any deficiencies in your process and assault any shortcomings that will get in your way.

If virtuous living—making decisions based on what's right, respectful and righteous—can meld with the virtual environment we embrace in today's world, with its smartphones and search engines, texting, apps and emails, websites, links and internet, then we would certainly be doing the ancient Greeks proud. Perhaps they would appreciate our efforts, congratulate us on our successes. They would respect our tenacity and marvel at our magnificent feats of modern-day technology. They would acknowledge and salute our failures and know them for what they are—learning opportunities. They would celebrate with us our lasting accomplishments.

Life is full of fleeting examples of virtue. Every day, throughout the world, on far-flung battlefields and on nearby street corners, in every city and every season, we have the opportunity to bear witness to human virtue, fighting the good fight.

So pay attention, and Warrior On.

APPENDIX

Notes on the
Warrior Mindset

"Do every act of your life as if it were the last act of your life."
—MARCUS AURELIUS, ROMAN EMPEROR

I N EXECUTING ANY plan of action, having the proper mindset is key. Without a clear head and a strong foundation of mental stability, even the best laid plans can go awry, especially in a traumatic or stressful situation. In cultivating a warrior's virtues, it also pays to actively develop a warrior's sense of tactical awareness, maintaining a perspective of capability, confidence and drive.

HABITS AND MINDFULNESS

A habit is an action executed consistently, regularly, routinely; like a strip of code in a piece of software, a habit becomes your programming, your algorithm for living. For a Marine, the rote exercise of stripping and cleaning your rifle is an exercise in discipline, one which serves as a mindfulness activity in disguise. The tools and the weapon become extensions of the warrior's body.

For civilians, one could make the analogy of a smartphone being an extension of one's body. You know where it is at all times, it typically never leaves your side, and you know how to operate it in all environments. We are aware of its benefits and become more present with it as we put it to use; when we are removed from it, it causes us stress in our lives.

Emotions often become attached to our habits, becoming the behavioral byproduct of those experiences, by way of having done them repeatedly. So, it follows that if you have had a collection of unvirtuous experiences, and you happen to recall these thoughts and emotions, your state of being is now trapped in reliving these old emotional states. It creates a moment where you are not aware, and disengaged from your current environment.

Mindfulness as a topic has been studied extensively over many years and has been incorporated by many business executives, celebrities, Ivy League institutions, professional sports teams, and elite military units around the world. It is the number one known tactic proven to reduce anxiety and depression. Extreme focus, clarity, and unrivalled achievement are just some of the residual benefits of improved mindfulness.

Being mindful means lingering in the present moment, devoid of past or future thinking. How we think and feel creates our entire state of being; our thoughts, behaviors, and emotions become circuits that fire in our brains, and that's the circuitry our body adopts. Through meditation and the tactics discussed in this chapter, you can make some really important changes to break these habitual behaviors and rewrite the programming that you have carried within yourself for so long. We all have the capacity for personal growth, but it is up to us to make the decision to work towards our goals.

Focusing on one single event or activity is difficult when we have a whole host of distractions being thrown at us. That's why we must learn to train the mind to be "right here, right now" at all times. When you are mindful, you have improved discipline, self-control and a head start on virtue. Many studies have shown that the earlier you can exhibit self-control and regulate your emotions in life, the greater the chances of personal mental and physical health, wealth, sustainable relationships and success.

Mindfulness is the warrior doctrine for absolute focus and learning. Implement these practices and adopt the mindset of a lifelong learner. Learning doesn't end in your senior year of high school or college; to be a warrior, you must be constantly learning. Having a warrior mind will positively impact your community, the people you work with and the people you live with. The following tactics will help you develop a warrior's mindful awareness.

MINDFULNESS TACTIC: BREATH CONTROL

In order to stay calm during anxious and stressful events, begin by minimize the pounding of your heart using a tactical warrior breath to bring you back into the action. Begin with a lower body inhale count of 1, 2, 3, 4, then breathe out to a count of four. Deep breathing starts at the lower belly. You breathe in for a count of four, you hold, and then breathe out. Picture a box. You go up to breathe in, across the top to exhale out, down the side of the box to inhale in, then exhale out at the base of the box.

Everyday routine tasks also provide an opportunity to develop mindfulness. Practice focusing your attention on sights, sounds, images, and the thoughts of the current moment. Whenever distraction creeps back in, bring yourself back to a very slow and deliberate focus on these simple sensory items. These everyday tasks will become a system of relaxation for you.

You can start off slowly, by introducing a few minutes of deliberate mindfulness here and there, slowly increasing over time. As you become adjusted to the routine and start to notice the benefits, begin to increase the amount of time and start experimenting with other daily activities.

A good place to start is by zeroing in on your breath control. The most important way for you to grab hold of the current moment is to have a lock on your breath. Without introducing any complexity to your breathing, begin by inhaling. Notice how it feels going in, then slowly exhale out. Notice how it feels going out and exiting the body. If your focus begins to slip, come back to your breath quickly and introduce a simple count of ten.

MINDFULNESS TACTIC: MEDITATION

If your routine task becomes too distracting, find yourself a quiet, comfortable place with dim lighting and sit in a position that is relaxing to you. Make sure to have your heels and toes flat on the floor, with your arms lying flat at your sides. Set an alarm for yourself if there's a fear you will fall asleep and miss your next task. Go ahead and close your eyes. Imagine a comfortable and relaxing place that you desire to be in at that moment. It may be a cascading pool at the edge of a skyscraper in Dubai, or a beautiful exotic beach with palm tree shade. Start to imagine the sights, sounds and feelings that may be attached to that "special place" of yours. Identify the specific sounds and feelings; see if you can feel the temperature of the air. Are you able to identify certain colors?

Now bring your breath into focus. Bring specific attention to the air flowing in through the nose, filling up the lungs, and then exhaling and exiting the body through the mouth. This full cycle can last anywhere from several seconds to a half a minute. Rinse and repeat, carrying out this cycle for 10–20 more times. You will start to feel a warmth accompanying the breath. As you get more comfortable with repeating these cycles, direct your breath and its warmth throughout the different parts of your body, slowly melting any tension away.

Let the top of your head be your starting point. Pay attention to the muscles that comprise your scalp and face. Bring a deep breath in and when you exhale the breath out, picture it filling up your head space and all the muscles attached. Use the warm air to melt and relax the tense spots in each and every one of the individual muscles. Then move down to your neck, shoulders and arms. Keep your eyes closed and make an attempt to arrive at your senses. Notice the textures, the smells and sounds.

When you first start to bring attention to your body, it is going to become very stressful. You are telling your body to be with itself, without changing. Just continue filling your lungs with breath, feeling as you exhale, feeling the sensation. Stay awake, alert and observant. Exhale; release your jaw and neck muscles, and work your way from your shoulders, to your torso, tightening and then quickly relaxing your muscles. Focus on your arms, buttocks, legs, and all the way down to the individual muscles in your feet and toes.

MINDFULNESS TACTIC: BODY SCAN

Use this warrior tactic whenever you have a free moment, or you find yourself sitting alone at your work desk. Always remember to focus on breath work and the tightening and releasing of muscles throughout your entire body. At the end of your mindful tactic, take an inventory of your entire body. Assess parts of the body that tend to be more tense than others. Try to identify which muscles or parts need more focus the next time around. The relaxed parts that find success will feel limp to you.

If you're having difficulty feeling the difference, try this. When you start at your head, you can scrunch up your forehead and close your eyes tight, or you can clench teeth and go through a series of facial features to flex your face. Your shoulders can be shrugged; your abdominal muscles can tighten, arms flexed by biceps and forearms. Your hands can be clenched fists. Then, working your way down to your buttocks you can tighten, lift and re-tighten your legs. Lastly, you can clench your toes as the last part of your body scan and relaxation tactic.

MINDFULNESS TACTIC: ANGER MANAGEMENT

Anger and rage can take some people a lifetime to chip away; for others it goes away gradually as we age. Self-help strategies and professional supports such as a therapy can also assist in long-term strategies of anger management. What is needed is an understanding that anger issues start with us, and we need to identify our shortcomings and fears and work towards bettering ourselves. Our fears can be faced by being exposed to them; our shortcomings can be worked on and our strengths can be accentuated. Once you learn the skills to identify and accept the "angry" behaviors in your life, you are well on your way to culti-vating a warrior's awareness. Remember, anger is a natural emotion, but if it escalates to rage it can have a severe impact on your life, your relationships, your employment and even your freedom.

When you feel yourself starting to get pissed off and angry at another person, it is time to slow things down and bring yourself back to a calm center. If you feel yourself being consumed with emotion and are failing to adapt and overcome the situation, refrain from responding. Pay attention to your emotions. Pay attention to the rapid changes in your body. If you are accelerating towards a state of real anger, swiftly move into your tactical breath-ing exercises.

A great way to get a handle on anger/rage incidents is to keep a journal. Identify the dates and times of said events. What was the initial trigger? Can you identify the feelings and emotions you were having during the event? Take a full inventory of your body and identify how it is feeling. Exactly how long did you stay angry? What was said? Are there any themes being repeated in your experiences? Make as many notes as possible.

MINDFULNESS TACTIC: JOURNALING

Warriors learn to challenge their negative core beliefs, and a great way to do so is by asking yourself specific questions and documenting the answers. Pay attention to your thoughts and feelings. Write down the feelings you are experiencing and then attach descriptive words to explain the experience. Describe your feelings as they come to you. Recognize the facts of the situation but place them off to the side. Instead, recognize the feelings attached to the situations.

Learn to assess the patterns that present themselves and perceive the reality of what you are feeling. Be accountable to yourself, and above all be attentive. Practice what you've learned throughout this book to become mindful, present and forward-facing.

Another way to use journaling to your advantage is to keep a record of your goals for the day. Try filling out a to-do list like the one on the following page.

By focusing the day on a single achievable goal, breaking down that goal into manageable steps, and setting a specific time, place and action plan for each of those steps, you'll instantly feel more in control of yourself and your schedule.

Warrior Goal-Setting: Plan for the Day _____

_____

Step 1: _____

Time: _____   Place: _____

Action: _____

Step 2: _____

Time: _____   Place: _____

Action: _____

Step 3: _____

Time: _____   Place: _____

Action: _____

Step 4: _____

Time: _____   Place: _____

Action: _____

Step 5: _____

Time: _____   Place: _____

Action: _____

Warrior Affirmations

- **Warriors don't avoid the important things they should be doing right now.** Drop your fears and excuses. They do nothing to help you.

- **Warriors are open minded and open to learning and understanding beliefs contrary to their own.** Be accepting and empathic to those different belief systems, as this is paramount to the warrior spirit.

- **Warriors commit to excellence**. Strive to raise your personal standards on a regular basis.

- **Warriors never, ever submit to the world and its problems**. They are committed to themselves, their quality and consistency.

- **Warriors always choose bravery over recklessness.** They work on developing their self-confidence, always speak the truth and make the commitment to stop apologizing.

- **Warriors practice what they preach.** Always speak your own truth.

- **Warriors know to pick their battles.** Continue to learn and identify your own personal triggers and learn to retreat from situations of weakness.

✅ **Warriors are prepared.** Focus on warrior preparation, focus on being good, and invest in yourself by working hard and promoting your own personal brand.

✅ **Warriors are architects of change.** Continue to adjust the way you see yourself by gathering information, data and intel.

✅ **Warriors stay focused**. Stay motivated and stay dedicated. Understand that nothing of great value comes quickly.

✅ **Warriors are comfortable with saying, "No."** One of the biggest chinks in a warrior's armor is a "Yes" at the wrong time and place.

✅ **Warriors are in it for the long haul.** Learn to kill off the desire for instant gratification and get away from all the distractions it brings.

✅ **Warriors incorporate physical fitness as a lifelong commitment**. That means staying in shape isn't something that ends with youth—there's no graduation from taking care of yourself. Being at peak physical fitness equips the warrior to better operate in chaos.

✅ **Warriors take care of themselves**. In order to be able to take care of the person on the left and right of them, warriors commit to being ready for anything.

Marine Corps Character Traits

- Integrity
- Justice
- Enthusiasm
- Bearing
- Endurance
- Unselfishness
- Loyalty
- Judgment
- Tact
- Initiative
- Dependability
- Decisiveness
- Courage
- Knowledge

Marine Corps Core Values

- Honor
- Courage
- Commitment

Plato's Cardinal Virtues

- Prudence
- Justice
- Temperance
- Fortitude

Marine Corps Leadership Principles

- Be technically and tactically proficient.
- Know yourself and seek self-improvement.
- Know your Marines and look out for their welfare.
- Keep your Marines informed.
- Set the example.
- Ensure the task is understood, supervised, and accomplished.
- Train your Marines as a team.
- Make sound and timely decisions.
- Develop a sense of responsibility among your subordinates.
- Employ your unit in accordance with its capabilities.
- Seek responsibility, and take responsibility for your actions.

Glossary of Terms

All Hands: Naval shorthand for "All Hands On Deck," meaning for everyone to come together to carry out a task

Anxiety: Symptoms of worry and concern, frequently regarding the unknown

APC: Armored Personnel Carrier

ASAP: Abbreviation for "As Soon As Possible"

As You Were: A military command meaning to go back to what you were doing

AWOL: Army term, meaning Absence Without Leave

BCE: Before the Common Era, referring to the time period prior to year 0 in the Gregorian calendar

Battalion: A ground force unit consisting of a headquarters and two or more companies or similar units, with both tactical and administrative functions

BAS: Battalion Aid Station

Bearing: Bearing is the manner in which one carries oneself. Military bearing is possessing or projecting a commanding presence and a professional image of authority. Bearing also describes appropriate behavior and demeanor for an event, at the appropriate time in the right place.

Bulkhead: Naval terminology for a wall

CACO: Casualty Assistance Calls Officer; the official representative of the Secretary of the Navy, they are tasked with notifying family (next of kin) and friends in person when their enlisted loved ones are killed or injured in the line of duty.

Carry On: A military command meaning to continue what you were doing

Chit: An official military note or memorandum of understanding.

Commitment: Held to the highest standards of dedication and obligation

Courage: Committed to the act of doing right in the face of fear or death

Cordite: Smokeless propellant used in military explosives; produced in Great Britain

DI: Drill instructor; usually a non-commissioned officer or staff commissioned officer tasked with training new recruits and molding them into young Marines

Discipline: The Marine Corps defines discipline as the "willful obedience to all orders, respect for authority, self-reliance, and teamwork"

Decisiveness: The ability to make sound decisions with swiftness and assuredness

Dependability: Being relied upon

Depression: Having self-doubt and feelings of dejection; chronic inability to experience pleasure; an unexplained loss of interest in once pleasurable activities; sadness that doesn't go away

Endurance: The ability to sustain and withstand difficult and unpleasant events

Enthusiasm: Having *esprit de corps* and intense joy and pleasure for what you are doing and what you are trying to accomplish

Faith: Trust without reservation

Feint: A movement made in order to deceive an adversary

Force Reconnaissance: Force Recon, for short; Marine Corps-trained personnel responsible for evaluation and gathering info/intel ahead of a unit assault; the USMC equivalent to a Navy SEAL

Fortitude: The ability to 'buck up,' to summon one's courage; being afraid and going into the hornet's nest anyway

Garrison: The collective term for a body of troops

Hatch: Naval terminology for an opening in a deck and/or a door. Hatches are a staple of ships, tanks, tactical vehicles and Naval and Marine Corps buildings.

Head: Naval terminology for a bathroom

Honor: To act with dignity and integrity

Hope: A fervent wish for a positive outcome or end result; confident expectation. A future-driven assurance of a promise to be fulfilled.

IED: Improvised Explosive Device. The signature weapon of insurgents in Iraq and Afghanistan, IEDs are low-cost bombs that can be modified to exploit specific vulnerabilities of an enemy. They range in size from a soda can to a tractor trailer and are initiated by anything from a pressure sensor to a suicidal attacker.

Initiative: The ability to act on your own, assess the situation and take charge

Integrity: To act with virtue and make the right decision even when someone isn't looking

Judgment: To make good sound decisions and think with a warrior mind

Justice: Fairness; one of the four Cardinal Virtues. Although it has been referenced in positive and negative terms in modern society, justice, in its proper sense, is a positive attribute.

Kalashnikov/AK-47: An assault rifled developed in the former Soviet Union by Mikhail Kalashnikov; weapon of choice for non-NATO countries and the former Warsaw Pact

Knowledge: Insight; warriors achieve knowledge through intel, information, facts, a honed skill-set and a mastery of a discipline

Loyalty: A strong allegiance and support to a select group of people, an organization, and or a loyal cause

Mindfulness: The warrior doctrine for absolute focus and learning

Oorah: *Kill* in Swahili; the United States Marine Corps battle cry, mid-20th century to present. Comparable to hooah in the U.S. Army and hooyah in the U.S. Navy and U.S. Coast Guard; most commonly used in response to a greeting or as an expression of enthusiasm.

Parris Island: MCRD (Marine Corps Recruit Depot)" Located in Beaufort County, South Carolina, USA, a Boot Camp for young men and women enlisting in the Marine Corps who live east of the Mississippi River. (All those living west of the Mississippi River attend San Diego, California USA, MCRD.)

Passageway: Planks or the sides of a ship where troops pass by

Police: Military term for cleaning the immediate area, to "police call"; pick up and clean

Porthole: Naval terminology for windows on a ship

Prudence: Care, caution, and good judgment, as well as wisdom in seeing ahead

PT Gear: Physical training attire

Sea bag: a canvas bag, closed by a line threaded through grommets at the top, used by seamen and other military personnel for belongings/possessions

Seabees (U.S. Navy): U.S. Navy Construction Battalion (CBs), a unit that deploys and builds in the theatre of war; they can shoot their rifles or their nail guns

Stoicism: An ancient Greek philosophy which teaches the development of self-control and fortitude as a means of overcoming destructive emotions

Square Away: Military terminology to sort out and fix

Tact: Being sensitive, thoughtful and considerate to others when delivering information

Temperance: Moderation in action, thought, feeling or restraint; one of the four Cardinal virtues

Toys For Tots: United States Marine Corps Reserve program that helps with literacy and delivers toys to those children in need during Christmas

Track: Short for a tracked and lightly armored vehicle, typical as part of a military operations ambulance crew

Trauma: Distress or injury from certain disturbing life events

UA: Unauthorized Absence

Unselfishness: Prioritizing concern for others over yourself

U.S. Marine Corps: A branch of the United States Military Services and department of the U.S. Navy, the Marine Corps was founded on 10 November 1775 at Tun Tavern, Philadelphia, Pennsylvania. The U.S. Marines fight in air, on land and at sea.

U.S. Navy: Military branch with roots to the Continental Navy; founded a month prior to the United

States Marine Corps. The U.S. Navy has the largest fleet of ships on the globe.

VBIED: Vehicle-Borne Improvised Explosive Device, also known as a car bomb. An explosive device carried by a vehicle and then detonated.

Virtue: Having the highest possible moral standing

Warrior: (noun) brave fighter; a person who shows great courage or vigor; (verb) to do battle and make better decisions when called upon; to cultivate just and virtuous lives. Warriors are expected to adapt to less than desirable circumstances and overcome obstacles.

XO: Executive officer

Selected Bibliography

Annapolis, MD: Naval Institute Press, 1984.

Armadilloze. (2006, December 09). Symbolically, White House Tree Falls – Olbermann Reports.

Baltes, P. B. (1999). Wisdom: The orchestration of mind and virtue. Book manuscript, Max Planck Institute for Human Development, Berlin, Germany.

Biddick, B. (n.d.). Get Up Nation Podcast. Retrieved 2018, from https://www.getupnationpodcast.com/

Holiday, R., & Hanselman, S. (2017). The Daily Stoic Journal. Portfolio/Penguin, New York, New York.

Holiday, R., & Hanselman, S. (2016). The Daily Stoic. London: Profile Books.

Johnson, P. (2011). *Socrates: A Man For Our Times*. London: Viking Penguin. [Html]. (n.d.). Retrieved November 9, 2018, from www.philosophybasics.com.

Shaw, L. (2005). *The Crime of Living Cautiously: Hearing God's Call to Adventure*. Downers Grove, IL: InterVarsity Press.

Hsei-Yung, H. (2016). *The Ancient Greek Concept of Justice: The Moral Values and Political Ideals from Homer to Aristotle* (First ed.). National Taiwan University Press.

Marcus Aurelius, *Meditations*

Plato, *The Republic*. New York: Books, Inc., 1943. Print.

United States Marines Corps. (2018). Retrieved from www.marines.com.

Washington, G. (1788). A Letter to Alexander Hamilton. Retrieved from founders.archives.gov/documents/ Washington/04-06-02-0432.

About the Authors

Nick Benas, USMC, is a former United States Marine Sergeant and Iraqi Combat Veteran. Author of *Mental Health Emergencies: A Guide to Recognizing and Handling Mental Health Crises* and *Tactical Mobility*, Nick travels around the United States training individuals on how to respond to emergency mental health situations. Nick attended Southern Connecticut State University for his undergraduate degree in Sociology, and for his M.S. in Public Policy. He has been featured in more than 50 major media outlets for his business success and entrepreneurship, including *Entrepreneur Magazine, Men's Health*, ABC, FOX, ESPN, and CNBC.

Matt Bloom, USMC, enlisted in the United States Marine Corps Reserves where he spent eight years and completed two combat tours to Iraq. During this time, he worked at a drug and alcohol rehabilitation facility as a counselor and assistant therapist for incarcerated offenders. Matt then worked as law enforcement at the Department of Veterans Affairs, then worked five years as a licensed social worker. Matt is currently a police officer in Pittsburgh, PA. Born and raised in western Pennsylvania, he attended Penn State University and has a Bachelor of Science degree in Criminal Justice, as well as a master's degree in social work (MSW) from the University of Pittsburgh.

Richard "Buzz" Bryan, USN, is currently the Outreach Coordinator for the West Palm Beach VA medical center. He previously served as the OEF/OIF Transition Patient Advocate (TPA) for the Veterans Integrated Service Network (VISN4) based in Pittsburgh, PA for ten years, working specifically with Iraq and Afghanistan veterans who were seriously injured/ill. Buzz was a dedicated and driven member of the Navy/Marine Corps team and retired from the United States Navy in July 2011 after 22 years of honorable service to the Fleet Marine Force.